Cricket
A Very
Peculiar
History™

With added googlies

'To stay in, you've got to not get out.'

Geoffrey Boycott,
Yorkshire and England cricketer

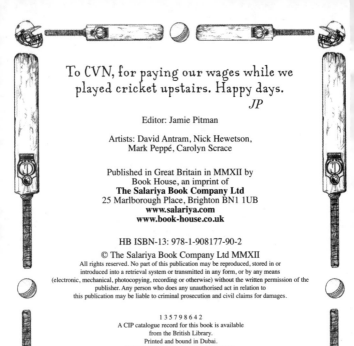

To CVN, for paying our wages while we
played cricket upstairs. Happy days.
JP

Editor: Jamie Pitman

Artists: David Antram, Nick Hewetson,
Mark Peppé, Carolyn Scrace

Published in Great Britain in MMXII by
Book House, an imprint of
The Salariya Book Company Ltd
25 Marlborough Place, Brighton BN1 1UB
www.salariya.com
www.book-house.co.uk

HB ISBN-13: 978-1-908177-90-2

1 3 5 7 9 8 6 4 2
A CIP catalogue record for this book is available
from the British Library.
Printed and bound in Dubai.
Printed on paper from sustainable sources.

Visit our website at **www.book-house.co.uk**
or go to **www.salariya.com**
for **free** electronic versions of:
You Wouldn't Want to be an Egyptian Mummy!
You Wouldn't Want to be a Roman Gladiator!
You Wouldnt Want to Join Shackleton's Polar Expedition!
You Wouldn't Want to Sail on a 19th-Century Whaling Ship!

Visit our **new** online shop at
shop.salariya.com
for great offers, gift ideas, all our new releases
and free postage and packaging.

Cricket
A Very
Peculiar
History™

With added googlies

Written by
Jim Pipe

Created and designed by
David Salariya

❛Cricket to us was more than play, it was a worship in the summer sun.❜

Edmund Blunden,
English poet, author and critic

❛Cricket needs brightening up a bit. My solution is to let the players drink at the beginning of the game, not after. It always works in our picnic matches.❜

Paul Hogan, Australian actor and comedian

Contents

A few reasons to play or watch cricket

- You get all the benefits of the great outdoors, safe in the knowledge that if it starts to rain, you can leg it indoors along with everyone else on the pitch.
- Cricket is tailor-made for the born idler, one of the few pastimes where a whole game can go by without actually having to do anything. While your colleagues are batting, it's perfectly acceptable to put your feet up or doze off (England cricketer Phil Tufnell was nicknamed 'the cat' due to his nap-taking abilities in the dressing room).
- Unlike any other game ever invented, cricket always stops for tea. This pause for rest, repast and reflection is fundamental to the game's civilising influence on players and fans.
- The satisfaction of hitting the ball clean out of the ground, skittling out rival batsmen or plucking the ball from mid-air for a spectacular catch lives in the mind for days after.
- Not just a retreat from the dull cares of life, cricket instills a range of Zen-like qualities: endless patience, the strength to endure the slings and arrows of outrageous fortune, and the grace to ignore a barrage of insults while at the crease.
- Picturesque cricket grounds abound. Breathe in all that scenery, from fields of sheep to centuries-old churches, while the wind whispers sweet nothings in the trees nearby.

A few reasons not to play or watch cricket

- Cricket whites may be elegant, but running between the wickets with pads on is at best ungainly and at times comical.
- The 'noble game' is not all it's cracked up to be. Professional players shout and scream after a run out or for an LBW decision, throw a tantrum when they're given out, and whisper obscenities at opposition players.
- Sheer boredom. In 1947, England wicket-keeper Godfrey Evans once spent an hour and 37 minutes at the crease before scoring his first run, while in 1964 Indian bowler Bapu Nadkarni bowled 131 scoreless balls in a row. Yawn.
- Watching a match, Groucho Marx once famously quipped 'Say, when do they begin?' Some would say he should have asked, 'When do they finish?' The 'timeless' Test match between England and South Africa at Durban in 1939 was finally abandoned as a draw on the tenth day (after 43 hours of play) because England players had to catch their ship home.
- It's not really a team game. Playing for Aberdeenshire against West Lothian, Bermudan Alma Hunt took seven wickets for 11 runs then scored the 49 runs needed to win himself in just 25 minutes. Game over.
- Collecting the ball. In a pub league match in Devon, Paul Crabb of Ilfracombe had to chase a ball over a kilometre after it rolled down a steep hill. He brought it back by bus, after the driver kindly overlooked the fact he did not have the 46p fare.

> **‘Cricket is basically baseball on valium.’**

Robin Williams, American actor and comedian

> **‘Baseball has the great advantage over cricket of being sooner ended.’**

George Bernard Shaw,
Irish writer and playwright

> **‘I do love cricket – it's so very English.’**

Sarah Bernhardt, French actress

ANYONE FOR CRICKET?

W hy do people enjoy a sport where 22 players loaf about all day? Well…

It's simple. One player throws a ball, another tries to hit it. To win, all you have to do is score more runs than the opposition.

Yet complicated. With its many 'laws', baffling terminology and unusual scoring system, cricket is also a game of immense complexity and beauty, where skill, strategy and raw emotions combine to create a fever-

pitch atmosphere. Australian novelist Thomas Keneally called cricket 'a sort of mystery'. In the early 1930s, when Adolf Hitler decided to use the game to train his troops for war, he rewrote the laws to make them simpler. Clearly the action of a crazed madman.

It's dramatic. At its best, cricket is soap opera, with a stock of villains and heroes and regular instalments of melodrama, hysteria and nail-biting suspense.

And tribal. When Australia play England, national pride is at stake. When 260 million people sat down to watch India play Pakistan in 2004, patriotic feelings ran high.

It's varied. My own experience of playing cricket in a local league is straight out of an Agatha Christie novel: the gentle murmur of conversation around the village green, hefted agricultural strokes, ruddy-faced umpires draped with spare sweaters, and scones and cream in the pavilion. The only thing missing was a body laced with arsenic. A modern international, especially the spectacle enjoyed by India's passionate cricket supporters, is a

different beast altogether, a heady brew of thousands of baying spectators, a bowler racing in like an express train to launch a rock-hard missile at the batsman's head – and the potential for pandemonium if there's any controversy on the pitch.

Cricket also comes in several flavours: long-lasting five-day Test matches (which purists consider to be the only reputable sort), chewy one day matches with a set number of overs, and for those who like an instant hit, Twenty20 games where each side has just 20 overs to produce an orgy of runs.

It's unpredictable. When a match lasts for five days, acts of God are two-a-penny, from sudden downpours and bizarre fungal infections to pitch invasions by birds and insects. No wonder cricket has been a favourite with gamblers for hundreds of years. Even when the game slows to a snail's pace, there is always something going on, a subtle change in fielding positions, how a bowler varies his delivery, or the careful way a fielder rubs spit onto the ball to make it shine.

The English are not very spiritual people, so they invented cricket to give them some idea of eternity.

George Bernard Shaw

Yet, for all its charms, you'll sometimes hear the uninitiated refer to cricket as – gasp – 'boring'. Though beauty is in the eye of the beholder, sometimes the ill-informed beholder needs to face the facts: cricket is the second biggest spectator sport on the planet (soccer is the first), watched by a billion or so people, and played by millions in over 100 countries across the world. Once upon a time, it was even the national game of the United States.

So how did it all begin?

❛Novelty is the one quality required for Christmas games ... If a game is novel it is enough. To the manager of a toy department the continued vogue of cricket must be very bewildering. ❜

A. A. Milne, author of *Winnie-the-Pooh*

full contact cricket?

One 10th-century Norse bat and ball game, knatteleik, was played by the Vikings of Iceland. A dawn-to-dusk affair that attracted huge crowds from all over the island, it was one of the roughest games ever invented, and deaths were common:

- There were two teams with captains and probably dozens of players.
- The playing field was a flat ice-covered surface (possibly a frozen pond), with the players using tar and sand under the soles of their boots for traction. Loose balls inevitably skittered a long way over the ice.
- Batters swung at balls of leather or wood (no, the batting helmets weren't horned).
- Apparently the bat was thin enough to be broken in anger and mended on the spot.
- Body contact was allowed, with opposing players wrestling for control of the ball.
- The ball was hard enough to make an opponent bleed when thrown in anger. Hurled with enough force, it could knock over another player.
- Slagging opponents was a key part of the game (and still is), and several choice outbursts are recorded in Icelandic sagas.
- Despite the carnage, there were some limits. In Snorre's saga, one player, Tord Blig, is given a life ban due to his 'bad temper'.

CHAPTER ONE

BAT MEETS BALL

Our knowledge of cricket's origins is hazy at best. As a result, there are more theories about how it all started than you can shake a stick at. At the heart of the game lies a primeval instinct to bash things, which in the Stone Age was a pretty fundamental life skill.

All bat-and-ball games probably began with a spotty, cave-dwelling youth picking up a stick and whacking a stone or a lump of wood flung by another hairy apeman (has the game changed that much in 10,000 years?).

 15

As humans settled down and became altogether more civilised, rules emerged and alternative forms of the game evolved in various parts of the world.

If all this sounds a bit fuzzy, brace yourself for some rock solid evidence that weaves sex, magic and religion into the story. Way back in 2400 BC, inscriptions refer to a game the ancient Egyptians dubbed seker-hermat, or 'batting the ball'. In one magical text, written on the walls of a pyramid, the gods (no less) command the Egyptian pharaoh to cross the heavens and 'strike the ball' into the meadow of the sacred Apis Bull.

We have to wait another thousand years to learn the name of the first known batsman, Thutmose III, who in 1475 BC was immortalised on the walls of a shrine dedicated to the love goddess Hathor. The all-conquering pharaoh is shown holding a curved bat in one hand and a leather ball in the other, while two priests, arms upright, grasp a ball in their hands. The aim of the game, it seems, was to swat at and destroy the evil eye of Apopi, the serpent of chaos. Such

ceremonies, held on festival days in honour of certain goddesses, were probably held in secret in the dark confines of the temple. If not, we can only imagine the roar of the crowd as the pharaoh spanked evil over the nearest pyramid and into the next world.

Leather balls have also been found in several ancient Egyptian graves. Made of four to twelve segments, some have alternating colours, while others are all white. Pharaonic floodlit cricket? Probably not, though flooding was always a risk with the River Nile just a stone's throw away, the start of an enduring relationship between the game and the elements.

According to an ancient Armenian manuscript, a bat-and-ball game may have been played in the Middle East during the days of Jesus Christ. The sixth-century artefact, thought to be a translation of a much older document, tells a story in which young Jesus is apprenticed to a dyer. One day, the boy is asked to keep an eye on things while his master visits a client. Like any nine-year old, Jesus soon gets bored and skips off to play a

game of bat-and-ball with his friends. We learn little of Christ's batting or bowling technique, but apparently he was able to play the game while treading over water 'as if it were a frozen surface'. This story will only reinforce the views of fans who regard the game as sacred (and whose heroes still walk on water).

The Middle Eastern connection appears in another recent theory, which suggests that a version of cricket was played by warriors in the Greater Punjab region (straddling modern north India and Pakistan), then headed west thanks to bands of nomadic Gypsies who wandered away from the Indian deserts through Persia and Turkey into Eastern Europe. Chess probably arrived in Europe via this route, so who knows?

fancy a game of stoolball?

Many historians believe that stoolball is the common ancestor of both baseball and cricket. It was certainly the first bat-and-ball game known to have been played in North America (at Plymouth in 1621 at Christmas, much to the annoyance of Governor William Bradford).

The sport dates back to at least the 15th century and originated in Sussex. Some experts say that 'stool' meant stump in the local dialect, but let's go with the popular myth that it was traditionally played by milkmaids who used their milking stools hung from a post or tree as a 'wicket'. The origins of the game have been linked to fertility rites, and in Shakespeare's day the phrase 'playing stoolball' was said with a nod and a wink.

Various language experts have traced the modern game of cricket to France, Holland, Germany, Libya and Spain, so take your pick! A mixed bag of bat-and-ball pastimes were certainly played throughout Medieval Europe, often as entertainment after the main service at religious festivals. The Church often encouraged these games, perhaps because it stopped villagers getting into other sorts of mischief on holy days.

Some survived into the 19th century, with names like 'kit-cat', 'tip cat' and 'cat and dog'. Animal lovers fear not, there's no evidence that any real animals were harmed during the match. Victorian 'cricketing gentleman' William South Norton noted that in 'Cat and Dog' two holes were dug 26 feet (about 8 metres) apart. A batsman armed with a bat called a 'dog' attempted to hit a piece of wood called a 'cat', while the bowler's aim was to get the cat into the hole.

If one place can claim to be the cradle of the modern game, it's probably the south-east of England, especially Kent and Sussex. It's time to put on your rose-tinted spectacles, to

imagine a rustic idyll where shepherds invented the game as a way of passing time while watching their flocks graze in verdant pastures. There's no hard evidence of course, but they certainly had motive, opportunity and the right tools at hand.

A shepherd's crook was a makeshift bat, and a solid-enough ball could be fashioned from a mix of matted wool and the coloured wax smeared onto a ram's chest to show if and when it had mated with a particular ewe (some have argued this is why cricket balls are traditionally red). Last but not least, the entrance to a sheep pen, a wicket gate, made a perfect target for a bowler to aim at.

Whether the shepherd story is true or not, by Tudor times cricket is recognisable as today's game. Back then, it was considered a silly game for school children, not to be played by serious-minded adults. In 1598, John Derrick, a coroner from Guildford, Surrey, refers to a game called 'creckett' which he played as a lad in the 1550s. The bat was a stick, curved at the bottom, designed to deal with a 'grass-cutter' bowled underarm along the ground.

21

Creag, crekette or sgrittare?

Academics have long batted around theories of where the word 'cricket' came from. To impress your friends, each version is best said with a heavy accent and the regionally-appropriate gesticulation:

- **Cric.** The medieval English word for the hooked staffs carried by shepherds.
- **Criquet.** The quintessential English pastime a French game? Surely not! Mais oui – there's historical evidence that a bat-and-ball game was being played in Northern France in 1478, and in old French, 'criquet' meant a post or a wicket.
- **Creag.** In the Wardrobe Accounts of the English Royal Household for the year 1300, a sum of 100 shillings were spent on 'creag' and other sports enjoyed by Edward I's son. Though the word could simply mean fun, as in the Irish 'craic' (pronounced 'crack') still widely used today.
- **Crekette.** A recent theory suggests the word originated in Flanders. Exhibit A is a poem written in 1553 by John Skelton, who calls emigrant Flemish cloth-workers in southeast England, 'kings of crekettes'. Given that Belgium has also given the world such wonders as the saxophone, chips and waffles, it's not beyond the bounds of reason.
- **Sgrittare.** In 1598, Florio's Italian–English dictionary defined the word *sgrittare* as 'to play cricket-a-wicket and be merry'.

Cricket gets serious

Early in the 17th century, people learned how to spell and 'cricket' was born (though hardly fully-formed). By now it was an adult game, played at a local level by peasants and all sorts of local scallywags. As it grew in popularity, so the arrest tally mounted. In 1613 Nicholas Hockley was charged in Guildford for attacking Robert Hewett with a 'cricket staffe', and in 1624, Jasper Vinall became the first cricketer known to have been killed while playing the game. He was walloped on the head by the batsman swiping madly at the ball a second time to avoid being caught out.

At the end of the English Civil War in 1648, the sound of leather on willow was muted by the arrival of the new Puritan government. These party-pooping Protestants were the folks who banned Christmas, so it should come as no surprise that they cracked down on any sport played on Sundays (pretty much a complete ban as it was the one free day in the week for most people). It was a mite hypocritical given that the Puritans were led by Oliver Cromwell, who had a reputation in

his youth as a 'royster' (bad-boy) for playing – you guessed it – sports such as cricket.

The game got a new lease of life when fun-loving King Charles II was restored to the throne in 1660. It attracted gamblers like moths to a flame. Cricket became fashionable among the gentry, who liked nothing better than a flutter, and cricket clubs began to proliferate. The game became a favourite in public houses, a traditional hotbed of gambling.

Pub landlords often sponsored the matches, as special beers brewed for the game weren't taxed, making the sport a big hit even with spectators unfamiliar to the game. Some gamblers formed their own teams to improve their chances of winning. The dangerous mix of drink and large wagers inevitably led to brawls and riots, and the first official record of a match was a legal tussle over the non-payment of wager on a game played at Coxheath near Maidstone, Kent, on 29 May 1646.

An ode to cricket

The first real description of the game was penned in 1706 by schoolmaster William Goldwin, who wrote the whole poem in Latin verse, titled: 'In Certamen Pilae' (On a Ball Game). Translated in 1922, it describes:

- A wicket that 'cries out for good defence' against 'the leather sphere'
- A fielder: 'a clearsighted scout prepares his ambush in the deep and with outstretched arms joyfully accepts it as it falls'
- A batsman who, going for a second run, 'falls headlong at the very foot of the wicket (as) the shaken earth groans beneath his great weight'.
- A win greeted by more than polite clapping: 'Victory... noisily flaps its wings and fills the sky with the shouts and roars of success'.

A match played in Devonshire Street in 1792, its windows an irresistible temptation to the incoming batsmen.

The game soon headed off on its first overseas tour, thanks to the sprawling British empire and its seafarers in particular. To a captain looking for a way to keep his crew amused in port, never-ending games of cricket must have seemed like a godsend. English sailors passed their love of the game on to the locals (along with a variety of nasty diseases that decimated several island populations).

Sailors almost certainly brought cricket to America. By 1705, colonists were already playing the game in New York, Boston, Georgia, Virginia and North and South Carolina. It was particularly popular among English settlers who considered themselves a cut above their neighbours. The first report of a cricket match in North America was in 1751, when the New York Gazette carried an account of a match between a London 'eleven' and one from New York City (though both sides were probably made up of locals).

In 1721, a report mentions English sailors of the East India Company playing a friendly match near Baroda, and by 1792 the first Indian club had been formed at Calcutta, one

of the oldest sporting clubs in the world. The earliest evidence of cricket in the West Indies is the famous Barbados Cricket Buckle, dating from the 1780s, which shows a batsman, wearing a slave collar, being bowled. Though the first recorded cricket match in Australia took place in Sydney in December 1803, it probably arrived with the first settlers in 1788, while the first known game in South Africa was played in 1808.

Back in Blighty, London was already a centre for cricket. Mitcham, a venue since the 1680s, claims to be the oldest cricket ground still in use and lists Admiral Nelson among its former spectators. By the mid-18th century, cricket had also caught on in many English towns and villages. The best players were drawn to clubs supported by wealthy patrons such as the Duke of Richmond.

The glamour team of the day was the Hambledon Cricket Club, created by Richard Nyren, landlord of the Bat & Ball Inn in Hambledon, Hampshire. Lords, politicians and well-known clergymen played alongside professionals like William 'Silver Billy'

Beldham. This 'village' team was good enough to beat the best in the land, winning 29 out of 51 matches played against an All-England side. Matches were major social events and huge sums were bet on the outcome.

The best village teams represented their county, the origins of the County Championship in England. When Kent took on an all-England team in 1744, at the Artillery Ground in Finsbury, London, it was the place to be seen. Kent won by one wicket, in what was hailed as the 'greatest match ever known'. A celebrity crowd came to watch, including the Prince of Wales, Frederick, the heir to the English throne. Cricket was getting serious – games once played for fun were now very much matches with lots of money and pride at stake. The well-heeled were separated from the common mob by ropes and guards. Unpopular results often ended in scuffles or even riots.

A pitch invasion by dogs at Hambledon led to a notice that in future dogs should be left at home – or they'd be shot!

Poor Fred

Frederick, Prince of Wales, the son of George II, was also a keen player who led Surrey in a game against London. In cricketing folklore, he died in 1751 after being hit on the head by a cricket ball (though in reality a burst abscess on his lung was to blame). His love of the game did not endear him to the masses, however, as this ditty written after his death reveals:

Here lies poor Fred who was alive and is dead,
Had it been his father I had much rather,
Had it been his sister nobody would have missed her,
Had it been his brother, still better than another,
Had it been the whole generation, so much better for the nation,
But since it is Fred who was alive and is dead,
There is no more to be said!

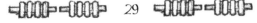

To minimise the risk of violence at the Artillery Ground (both on and off the pitch), a first stab was made at writing down the rules. Ten years later, these crossed the Atlantic when Benjamin Franklin returned home with a copy of the 1744 Laws packed in his trunk.

By the 1780s, cricket was a game for 'gentlemen'. In London, the upper classes played at White Conduit Fields in Islington, and big matches already lasted three days. Though cricket was regarded as a thoroughly butch activity, like shooting or fox hunting, the gentlemen batsmen sometimes hired lower class men to bowl to them, so they could look good thumping the ball into the distance with muscular grace. The class divide was replicated in public schools such as Harrow, Eton and Winchester. From 1806 to 1962, an annual match was played between amateur 'Gentlemen' from the schools and colleges and the professional 'Players'. The odds were usually in favour of the players, so to give the Gentlemen a chance they were allowed additional players.

The Gentlemen went one step further in 1787, creating a private cricket ground where they could play without being disturbed by noisy, vulgar crowds of commoners, setting a trend for elitist cricket clubs that hasn't completely died out. Backed by the Earl of Winchelsea, Thomas Lord, a professional player with the White Conduit club, formed a new club in the London district of Marylebone. The Marylebone Cricket Club (MCC), which became the daddy of all cricket clubs, hosted its first match between Middlesex and Essex on 31 May, 1787. Though it has moved twice since, the ground still bears its founder's name – Lord's.

To underline its importance, in 1788 the MCC wrote down the laws of cricket, covering everything from the measurement of the pitch to the weight of the ball. With a few small tweaks, the game was very much the sport we know today, and for the next 200 years the MCC was the game's unquestioned lawmaker.

Under, round and over

Cricket faced another crisis in the 1820s with the controversy over the introduction of overarm bowling. In the early days, bowlers rolled the ball along the ground. While bumps in the pitch might offer plenty of challenges for the batsmen, bowlers looked for other ways to outsmart their opponents, such as 'length' bowling, or bouncing the ball. Skilled bowlers like Edward 'Lumpy' Stevens could also make the ball spin and swerve in the air.

Today, underarm bowling is equated with gentle lobs. If you believe the tales, it was a very different story in the early 19th century. Hambledon's David Harris specialised in crushing a batsman's fingers against the handle of his bat, while George Brown 'of Brighton' bowled so fast that a fielder in line with the stumps insisted on having a sack of straw tied to his chest for protection. Brown is even said to have killed a dog after one bullet-like delivery shot past the batsman, wicket-keeper and through a coat held up by a fielder on the boundary.

Not everyone was happy to play by the MCC's rules. John Willes (1778–1852) bowled 'round-arm' (with his arm at elbow height) on and off until a match against the MCC in 1822. When his first delivery was called a 'no ball' (i.e. illegal), he threw away the ball, stormed off the pitch and supposedly never played again. But Willes was not alone, and umpires increasingly turned a blind eye to round-arm bowling. There's also a story that they began to wear white coats at this time, to help batsmen spot a speeding ball coming out of the bowler's hand.

In 1828, the MCC decreed that a bowler's hand should be no higher than the elbow when the ball was released. Within seven years, elbow became shoulder, and deliveries got faster still. Around this time, Nicholas 'Felix' Wanostrocht wrote his famous instruction book: *Felix on the Bat* (1845). In it, he recommended padding to protect the legs. (The Caractacus Potts of the cricketing world, Wanostrocht also invented the 'Catapulta', the world's first bowling machine, as well as India-rubber batting gloves).

In the 1850s, the demon bowler John 'Foghorn' Jackson appeared in several Punch cartoons, the comic element provided by the pained faces of village batsmen battered by one of his lightning deliveries. By 1864, overarm bowling was finally made legal, allowing players to hurl the ball down the pitch at increasingly ferocious speeds.

In 1844, cricket made history when a match between teams from the United States and Canada became the first international sporting event in the modern world, beating the modern Olympic Games by more than 50 years. In 1859, the English cricket team went on its first overseas tour, to North America, playing against teams of 22 to make games more evenly matched. The final game, played in New York State in October, was so bitterly cold that the fielders were allowed to wear gloves and overcoats.

The earliest first-class match in Australia was played in February 1851, between Tasmania and Victoria, and by the 1860s Australia was playing New Zealand. In 1877, England travelled to Australia for the first ever

fancy footwork

Bowlers weren't the only ones experimenting with new-fangled techniques:

- William 'Silver Billy' Beldham (1766–1862) was one of the first players to use his feet to attack bowlers – jumping two-footed to the pitch of the ball like a kangaroo. Though it sounds ludicrous today, at the time it was so effective there were fears that soon bowlers wouldn't be able to get batsmen out.

- William Fennex (1763–1838) came up with the idea of stretching his front foot forward to meet the pitch of the ball, creating the forward defensive stroke.

- Another innovation came by accident: the story goes that the 1948 Australian 'Invincibles' touring party were expected to ballroom dance in order to fulfil the social obligations of the tour. Apparently the footwork required for the quickstep was the perfect practice for quick feet out at the crease!

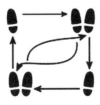

international Test match (it took seven weeks by ship). The match was played at Melbourne Cricket Ground. So began one of the most celebrated rivalries in international cricket.

The Australians won the match by 45 runs, helped by the fact that England had left their star player, W. G. Grace, at home. Meanwhile wicket-keeper Ted Pooley was flung in gaol after being arrested for fighting, while five other English players picked up a stomach bug on the boat over (a perennial hazard for touring sides, especially in India and Pakistan. English spinner Phil Edmonds once commented: 'What I look forward to most on returning from a tour of India is a dry fart').

A few years later, in 1882, Australia again beat England. It was a close match, with Australia winning by 8 runs in a nail-biting finish – the tension was so great one spectator is even said to have bitten through his umbrella handle. The defeat prompted an English writer to publish an satirical obituary in the Sporting Times for English cricket, claiming it was 'dead'.

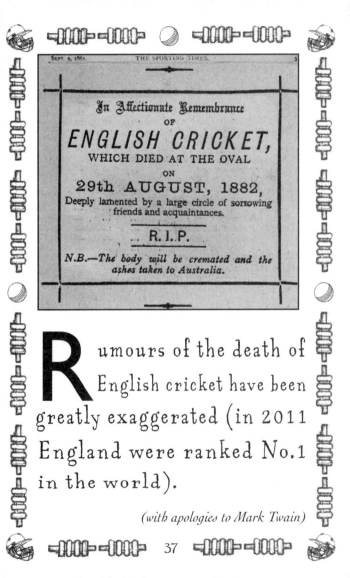

In Affectionate Remembrance

OF

ENGLISH CRICKET,

WHICH DIED AT THE OVAL

ON

29th AUGUST, 1882,

Deeply lamented by a large circle of sorrowing friends and acquaintances.

R. I. P.

N.B.—The body will be cremated and the ashes taken to Australia.

Rumours of the death of English cricket have been greatly exaggerated (in 2011 England were ranked No.1 in the world).

(with apologies to Mark Twain)

A global game

As the British empire stretched across the world, so the game of cricket spread with it.

- It was particularly popular with the Parsi community in Bombay who were sending touring teams to England by the 1880s. A decade later, Prince Ranji (K. S. Ranjitsinhji) hired a group of top-notch England players to coach him. It paid off, and in 1896 he was called up to play for England, scoring a century on his debut, and revolutionising the game with his scoring strokes off the back foot. The first-class cricket competition in India, the Ranji Trophy, is named after him.

- One of the fastest bowlers of the era was the great American cricketer J. Barton King, who set bowling records that stood for over 40 years in the 1908 tour of England. King developed special exercises to strengthen his wrist and fingers. Legend has it that he could flip a cricket ball up to a second-storey window with a snap of his fingers! Following the American Civil war, however, cricket was increasingly eclipsed by baseball (based on rounders – a game played by English schoolgirls it should be noted), which was faster, easier to learn, and needed little in the way of equipment.

- The first international not involving Australia was played between England and South Africa in 1889, the same year the South African national tournament, the Currie Cup, was founded. The English side was led by C. Aubrey Smith, who later became a Hollywood film actor famous for 'officer and gentlemen' roles. While fielding at slip for the Hollywood Club, so the story goes, Smith dropped a tricky catch and ordered his English butler to fetch his spectacles, which were carried on to the field on a silver platter. When the next ball flew straight at him and he dropped it, Smith excused himself, complaining, 'Damn fool brought my reading glasses'.

The following summer, England played another series against Australia. The English captain Ivo Bligh announced his side would 'regain the ashes', and the newspapers soon picked up on the idea. If you believe the legend, a group of Melbourne women burnt a cricket bail or stump and presented a small urn filled with ashes to the English captain. To this day, all test matches between England and Australia are said to be played 'for the Ashes'. The urn is never held aloft as a trophy – though it can be seen in the MCC Museum in London.

In England, the somewhat haphazardly organised county game began to take shape. Sussex became the first county club in 1839. A championship of sorts was held in 1864, in practice a very loose association of eight county clubs. 1895 saw the first proper County Championship, with points and a table, and by 1899, 15 counties were taking part. 1889 marked the first ever evening match, known as the 'Gaslamp Game'. The gaslamps in the pavilion at the Oval were turned on as the light faded in a match between Surrey and Yorkshire. These were a far cry from the blazing floodlights of today's stadiums, and in the dim haze one poor batsman's gloveless hands were battered and bruised by speeding balls he couldn't see.

Other firsts include the introduction of boundaries in 1884, preventing the use of nearby shrubbery to hide the ball, while in 1889 the four-ball over was replaced by a five-ball over, which became the current six balls in 1900 (though eight-ball overs were the norm in Australia and New Zealand until 1979).

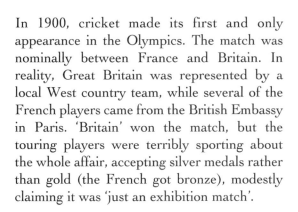

A cricketing heavyweight?

Despite being 1.68 m and weighing just 44.45 kg (possibly the lightest cricketer ever) in his debut match for Surrey, John Wisden certainly punched above his weight, becoming one of the finest all-round cricketers of his generation. Nicknamed the 'Little Wonder', he is still the only player to clean bowl all ten wickets in a first-class match. His real fame rests with the *Wisden Cricketers' Almanack*, however, the bible of cricket which he first published in 1864 (the longest running sports annual in history). The first edition had only 112 pages, but included the dates of battles in the English Civil War, the winners of The Oaks horse race.

In 1900, cricket made its first and only appearance in the Olympics. The match was nominally between France and Britain. In reality, Great Britain was represented by a local West country team, while several of the French players came from the British Embassy in Paris. 'Britain' won the match, but the touring players were terribly sporting about the whole affair, accepting silver medals rather than gold (the French got bronze), modestly claiming it was 'just an exhibition match'.

By the turn of the century, the tide was turning against the amateur game. Australia and India developed their own 'cadres' of full-time professional cricketers, and staged domestic tournaments (the Sheffield Shield in Australia, and the Pentangular in India) to promote homegrown cricket talent. The Imperial Cricket Conference (ICC) was formed in 1909, with England, South Africa, and Australia as the founding members. They were joined by the West Indies in 1928, New Zealand a year later, while India played its first test match in 1932.

In the past 50 years, Pakistan, Sri Lanka and Zimbabwe have joined the ranks of the major cricketing nations. Renamed the International Cricket Council in 1989, the ICC now has over 100 members and is responsible for organising all Test matches and one-day internationals as well as appointing umpires and referees.

The five day Test is the still the pinnacle of the game, though it's had its problems over the years, most notably the 'Bodyline Series' of 1932–33, when English bowlers hurled aggressive, short-pitched balls at the Australian batsmen. To prevent this tactic being repeated, the laws were changed to allow the umpire to intervene if they thought a bowler was deliberately trying to injure a batsmen.

In the 1960s, English teams began playing a shortened version of cricket that allowed a match to be completed in a day. Despite the objections of diehard fans and players who felt this went against the spirit of the game, English county teams took part in the first one-day knockout tournament in 1963 and in a league competition six years later.

The first limited-overs international match in 1971 was an accident, used as a time-filler after a Test match at Melbourne Cricket Ground had to be abandoned due to heavy rain on the opening days. One-day Internationals (or ODIs) soon became massively popular, as spectators could see a

whole game without having to take several days off work. The Cricket World Cup, first held in 1975, is played in this format.

The sport got a makeover in the late 1970s, after Australian media mogul Kerry Packer set up the rival World Series Cricket (WSC) competition. Though his tournament was branded a 'circus' or the 'stupid pyjama game' by critics, Packer revolutionised the game, ushering in coloured uniforms and floodlit evening matches played with a white ball, along with technical innovations such as multiple camera angles, microphones in the stumps, slow-motion replays and on-screen graphics, while ready-made pitches were grown in greenhouses outside the ground then lowered into place using cranes. For two seasons Packer recruited many of the top stars from England, Australia and West Indies, who played each other in 'supertests'.

Over the next 20 years, many of Packer's innovations became part of one-day and Test match cricket. In 1992, a third umpire was appointed to adjudicate runout appeals using television replays, later expanded to

include stumpings, catches and boundaries, controversially allowing players to challenge decisions made by the on-field umpires. In these 20 years, an array of hi-tech gadgets has also given armchair fans further insights into what has happened out on the pitch.

Cricket, now a billion-dollar sport with all the modern pressures of TV ratings, politics and a media circus around the players, has certainly come a long way since the bat-and ball games of medieval Europe and even the sport played by 18th-century 'gentleman amateurs'. Yet for all this, the game retains its unique spirit and sense of fair play.

This Sri Lankan five-rupee coin was issued in to celebrate winning the 1996 Cricket World Cup.

A safe haven?

Only in cricket do the players have a little cottage built for them to rest in. But this sanctuary is not always as safe as it seems:

- Pavilions are a favourite target for arson attacks in England, probably because of the game's reputation as a 'sport for toffs'. In 1913, Suffragettes burned down the pavilion at Tunbridge Wells, while in 2006 the Zimbabwean Test player Mark Vermeulen, furious that he had been left out of the national squad, set fire to the club which housed the Zimbabwe Cricket headquarters, destroying all the national equipment.

- When rain stopped play during a game at Taunton, Somerset in 2005, England batsman Mark Ramprakash headed for the pavilion for a cup of tea. Tripping over the steps, he dislocated a toe. Despite the pain, he later hobbled out to the crease to score a painful 11 runs.

- During the Centenary Test at Lord's in 1980, MCC members, frustrated by the decision to halt play until the pitch dried out, jostled and swore at umpires David Constant and Dickie Bird on the steps of the pavilion.

- In 2011, spectators sitting near the Lord's pavilion were showered with glass after a bat thrown by England wicket-keeper Matt Prior 'bounced off other bats' and broke the dressing room window.

THE FIELD OF PLAY

Just about anyone can play cricket, and with a little imagination, it can be played almost anywhere. In the Indian countryside, dried lakes and riverbeds are often used as cricket grounds. In cities, it is played in parks, parking lots, back alleys and apartment corridors.

In the professional game, creating a good wicket is one of the game's Holy Grails. When, in 2004, a soil expert from the ICC claimed the type of soil Bermuda used for its cricket pitches was 'more suitable for growing carrots', it was a huge blow to the island's

pride, sparking a long-running row over whether or not to bring soil in from abroad. In 2011, a decision was finally made for the local sod to stay put, after horrified local farmers recalled how alien bugs hitching a ride in imported soil had wiped out most of the island's cedar trees some 60 years before.

> **A cricket ground is a flat piece of earth with some buildings around it.**
>
> Richie Benaud, Australian cricketer

Cricket matches are played on a large, grassy and (ideally) flat field. If that sounds a bit vague, it's because cricket is about the only major sport where there's nothing in the rules stating exactly what size or shape the field needs to be – beautifully summed up in commentator Trevor Bailey's description of the Port Elizabeth ground in South Africa as 'more of a circle than an oval. It is long and square.' To give a rough idea of scale, the

largest ground in the world is currently Melbourne Cricket Ground, with a pitch measuring 174 metres by 149 metres, and seating for 100,000 spectators.

The earliest cricket grounds, such as Lord's, tended to be oval – the Oval in south London got its eponymous shape from a road built around it in the 1790s. Most modern grounds follow suit, though others are more circular or rectangular, while Eden Park in Auckland is a hexagon.

There are several distinct areas of the field. Those unfamiliar with the game should pay particular attention to the brown-coloured strip in the middle of the field, known as the pitch or wicket, where most of the action takes place. Pitches are 22 yards long (20.12 m) and 10 ft wide (3.05 m). If 22 yards seems like a random measurement, it's equivalent to a 'chain', which was once a popular unit of land measurement (it is still used to show the distance of a railway bridge along a line in England).

A veritable army of maintenance staff, marshalled by the head groundsman, lovingly mow, water, roll and shield the pitch from the weather, creating a spongy surface that's more like flattened mud than the lush grass on a lawn. In theory, a good wicket is as flat and smooth as a billiard table. Most billiard tables, however, are not subject to being trampled on by spiked boots or exposed to the elements. Over five days, wickets can became badly cracked, giving a helping hand to spin bowlers if they can land their delivery in the 'rough'. Such considerations have to be weighed up in the mind of a captain when deciding whether or not to bat first if he wins the toss.

The wicket sits in the middle of the 'square', a large rectangular area more manicured than the rest of the field. Outside this is the 'infield', everything within 30 yds (27.4 m) of the wicket. In limited overs matches, this is marked with a white line as there are restrictions on the number of fielders you can have outside this 'zone'. Beyond this is the outfield, which stretches out to the boundary, which is marked by a thick rope.

One of the curiosities of the game is the fact that every cricket ground has a particular feel of play to it. The hard, 'bouncy' pitches in Australia and the West Indies are made for fast bowlers and stroke-playing batsmen, for instance, while the slow, 'dry' wickets in India and Pakistan generally favour spin bowlers. The 'green' wickets of England and New Zealand are more suited to swing bowlers. Meanwhile, cutting the grass in the outfield longer or shorter leads to slower or faster pitches.

' He played his cricket
on the heath.
The pitch was full
of bumps.
A fast ball hit him
on the teeth,
The dentist drew
the stumps. **'**

Anon

Too dangerous

In 1998, a Test match was called off for the first time in 121 years, when umpires decided that the pitch at Sabrina Park in Jamaica was too dangerous to play on after just 62 wickedly bouncing, bone-crushing deliveries. The English physio had already been called onto the pitch six times in 66 minutes to tend to injuries.

Now for the science bit: climate and the ground's height above sea level affect how the ball moves through the air. For example, playing close to the sea is a boon to bowlers who swing the ball in the air, as they are aided by the salty sea air and unexpected gusts of wind. The greater pull of the Earth's gravity and the higher barometric pressure at lower elevations also come into play.

famous cricket grounds of the world

1. Old Trafford, Manchester
2. Headingley, Leeds
3. Trent Bridge, Nottingham
4. Lord's, London
5. The Oval, London
6. Jamaica, Caribbean
7. Trinidad, Caribbean
8. Barbados, Caribbean
9. Cape Town, S. Africa
10. Johannesburg, S. Africa
11. Harare, Zimbabwe
12. Sharjah, UEA
13. Karachi, Pakistan
14. Mirpur, Pakistan
15. Lahore, Pakistan
16. Mumbai, India
17. Chennai, India
18. Colombo, Sri Lanka
19. Chittagong, Bangladesh
20. Adelaide, Australia
21. Melbourne, Australia
22. Sydney, Australia
23. Christchurch, New Zealand
24. Wellington, New Zealand
25. Auckland, New Zealand

United Kingdom

Caribbean islands

Unlikely venues

There's a cricket pitch out there to suit all tastes. For many years, tree-huggers were naturally drawn to Kent's country ground at Canterbury, one of just two first-class cricket grounds with a tree within the field of play (the other being the Pietermaritzburg Oval in South Africa). If a ball hit the tree, it counted as four runs. In 1992, Carl Hooper became the last of just four players to hit a six over the tree, some 30 metres tall at its peak. Sadly, the 200-year old lime was 'stumped' after snapping in two during in a violent storm in 2005 (though a young tree was planted in the same spot a few months later).

Cricketers who yearn for the salty tang of the sea in their nostrils should head for what is probably the lowest ground in the world, the 'Brambles' sandbar in the Solent (the channel separating the Isle of Wight from the southern coast of England). Here the game is played just once a year at the end of summer, when the sandbank is briefly exposed during a low water spring tide.

A cricketing high

The world's highest ground is near the village of Chail, in Himachal Pradesh, India, a lofty 2,444 metres above sea level. It was built by the Maharaja of Patiala in 1893, whose passion for the game was such that he had a Himalayan hilltop leveled at great expense, giving spectacular views of snow-capped mountains from the crease.

Legend has it that prisoners from Parkhurst prison on the Isle of Wight were the first to play cricket on the bank, encouraged by a governor who thought that escape would be impossible. In the early 20th century, sailors are also said to have played cricket here using oars for bats, and today the tradition is continued by two sailing clubs – the Royal Southern Yacht Club and the Island Sailing Club.

Occasionally the tide doesn't go out far enough to allow for a proper match. In 2008, the waves never sank below the players' knees. Even in a good year, the lumpy surface and decidedly soggy outfield mean that serious cricket is a non-starter, so the two teams sportingly take it in turns to 'win' the match, regardless of what actually happens on the field of play.

Hardy types should note that in 1878–79, one of the coldest British winters on record led to a new sport – cricket on ice. Students from Cambridge University took on the 'Townies' on the flooded Grantchester meadows, which had frozen over. Most of the players wore ice skates, and after three days' play the ice became badly rutted, creating a decidedly tricky batting track. Fast deliveries were banned and as it was nigh impossible to make the ball turn on the ice, bowlers relied on a change in pace to outwit their opponents. However, as one player commented in *The Times*: 'Fielding was delightful, and the chase of the ball into "space" when it eluded you most exhilarating.'

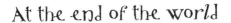

At the end of the world

Each February 12, the founding date of the Australian Antarctic Research Station, Australian scientists take on all-comers in a sub-zero cricket match played on the base's concrete helipad. Local rules apply:

- Any ball ricocheting off the Red Shed (the two-storey living quarters) scores four runs.
- Over the roof is six.
- Hit the station leader at the barbecue and you're out.
- Any fielder who lets the ball through faces a trek down treacherous icy slopes to fetch the ball from a small meltwater lake.

The slippery sport caught on in other parts of England. One moonlit match took place on the frozen floodwaters at Windsor Park, and several hundred spectators came to watch. 'The game caused no end of amusement owing to the difficulties encountered by the players while bowling, batting and fielding,' reported Wisden. Today, the game of ice cricket is still played in countries such as Estonia, Switzerland and the Netherlands. Red composite balls are used, as they're easy to find in snowdrifts.

Sun-worshippers will relish the ground at Sharjah in the United Arab Emirates, built in an oasis in the middle of a desert. When Pakistan hosted Australia in two Tests at Sharjah in 2002, the temperatures reached a scorching 50° C. The heat isn't the only hazard – in April 1998, a massive sandstorm swept across Sharjah from nowhere, sending players and the 22,000 crowd running for shelter. The one-day game between India and Australia was interrupted for about half an hour, and when it restarted, Indian run-monster Sachin Tendulkar dusted himself off and smashed 143 runs in double-quick time in his famous 'sandstorm innings'.

> ❛ Oh God! If there be cricket in heaven let there also be rain. ❜

Alec Douglas-Home, British Prime Minister (1963–1964) and cricketer

Cricketus interruptus

Cricket is a game famously at the mercy of the elements. It's not just rain and poor light that sends players back to the pavilion. Fog is a common problem in Pakistan, to the point where it's been suggested to add an extra day to Test matches to allow for this common intruder. In 1998, a Test match between Pakistan and Zimbabwe had to be completely abandoned after the ground was wrapped in a blanket of fog for the first four days.

2 June 1975 started off as a sunny summer's day in the town of Buxton, Derbyshire (at 365 metres above sea level, England's highest town), but by mid-morning a freakish blizzard had covered the wicket in an ankle-deep layer of snow. Umpire Dickie Bird wasted no time in abandoning the match for the day, the only time in the history of first-class cricket that snow has stopped play. The West Indian captain Clive Lloyd, who grew up in tropical Guyana, couldn't resist lobbing a few snowballs at his team mates – it was the first time he had ever seen snow.

Expect the unexpected

Pulling on a cricket sweater seems to be a sure way of summoning a freakish natural disaster:

- During the 1972 Ashes contest, the fourth test at Headingley became known as the 'Fusarium Test' after the fungus killed the grass on the pitch following a freak storm a few days earlier.
- In November 1937, *The Times* reported that two minutes were lost during an unofficial Test between Lord Tennyson's XI and India at Lahore when 'the ground was rocked for 90 seconds by an earthquake'.
- During a match between Yorkshire and Gloucestershire at Sheffield in July 1953, the fielders were forced to run for cover after lumps of ice rained down on the pitch (probably caused by an aircraft jettisoning waste water at high altitude).
- In 1995, a game being played in Gloucestershire was officially abandoned by the umpires after thick black smoke from a nearby animal crematorium blanketed the ground.
- Mercifully, lightning-strikes on cricket grounds are rare. During the 1954–55 Currie Cup, however, when Rhodesia hosted Eastern Province, several fielders were thrown to the ground and the scorers' box burst into fire after electrical equipment blew up following a direct hit from a lightning bolt.

The game has also been plagued by a variety of beasts, creeping things and winged fowl. Donkeys, bulls, dogs, pigs, sparrows, hedgehogs, mice, a large iguana and a troupe of circus camels have all stopped play over the years. In December 1951, a monkey nicknamed 'Jacko' apparently took up fielding position at midwicket before being chased off the pitch in a match between the MCC and the Indian state of Maharashtra.

In October 2009, a pesky swarm of flying ants disrupted play during the ICC Champions trophy in South Africa, while in 1962 a swarm of bees sent players scurrying to the pavilion in a game between Oxford University and Worcestershire. One match in England's 1922–23 tour of South Africa saw the pitch invaded by small green frogs. Play came to a complete halt until the groundsmen were able to usher them to safety.

Players have reacted to such intrusions in very different ways. In June 2002, India's Sachin Tendulkar and Sri Lanka's Mahela Jayawardene tenderly carried an injured pigeon struck by a ball off the field.

In contrast, when a brown snake emerged from its underground nest during a game in South Australia in 1967, the batsman swiftly beat it to a pulp with his bat. However, play was further delayed while the wicket-keeper returned to the field, having taken fright and legged it to the pavilion.

One of the highlight's of the MCC museum is a stuffed sparrow. It is forever stapled to the ball that killed it, hit by Jehangir Khan in a match at Lord's in 1936 between the MCC and Cambridge University.

I thought a 'birdie' was something you got in *golf!*

A welcome break

Unless they're in the midst of knocking up a big score, most cricketers welcome the interruption of lunch and tea (40 minutes and 20 minutes respectively during a Test match). This tradition harks back to the great feasts enjoyed by noble spectators in the early days of the game, with peckish players soon getting in on the act. The food on offer is often very different for amateurs and professionals. Club cricket lunches are all about filling up on sandwiches, crisps and sausage rolls, while meals for professionals focus on energy and nutrition.

❝ We used to eat so many salads, there was a danger of contracting myxomatosis. ❞

England cricketer Ray East

food, glorious food

If you are what you eat, what can we learn from the diets of cricketers?

- Victorian cricketer Alfred Mynn once famously scolded a young cricketer for drinking tea, saying that 'beef and beer are the thing to play cricket on'.

- Ham and lettuce were the staple foods for professionals for many years, causing West Indian cricket legend Garry Sobers to declare that no one could call himself a cricketer until he had eaten a ton of lettuce.

- Notable exceptions were the meals served up by Nancy Doyle, châtelaine of the players' dining-room at Lord's in the 1980s and early 1990s. Her belt-busting lunches caused England captain Mike Brearley to ask (unsuccessfully) if she could limit the number of courses to five.

- According to Steve Waugh, Glenn McGrath ate the same breakfast each morning on tour. After placing his two fried eggs on separate pieces of white toast (making sure the yolk was perfectly positioned in the middle), he then trimmed the overhanging egg white edges with surgical precision. The contents were then cut into quarters after being sprayed with salt.

- Australian wicket-keeper Ian Healy once quipped that 'Shane Warne's idea of a balanced diet is a cheeseburger in each hand.' During the Australian tour of India in 1998, Warne opted for a diet of baked beans and tinned spaghetti instead of the local curries. Hearing of his request, Heinz shipped out 2,000 tins for the whole team.

- After England bowler Bob Willis accused a particular Australian beer of tasting like 'weasel's piss', he and Ian Botham were persuaded by Australian winemaker Geoff Merrill to come up with a new wine, marketed as BMW (Botham-Merrill-Willis).

- During the 2011 World Cup, held in India, Sri Lanka and Bangladesh, two policemen worked as official food tasters to protect the Indian and Pakistani cricket teams ahead of the semi-final clash, eating three lavish meals a day at the luxury Taj hotel in Chandigarh to check for poisoning or other hygiene problems.

It's not a ton, but it's a start!

Smash hits

Cricket and smashed windows are like horses and manure – one invariably leads to the other. But spare a thought for the neighbours.

- In 2010, a villager from St Helens on the Isle of Wight saw red after a cricket ball struck his window for the fifth time. Leaping into his car, he drove onto the pitch, sending players and umpires scampering. After parking the vehicle on the wicket, he refused to budge until he got an apology from the team.

- In 2011, the Pacific Cricket Club in Islington, London was banned from playing by the local council after a ball smashed the window of a neighbour's Porsche. Apparently this resulted from a long-running spat in which the owner of the car grabbed any cricket balls that landed anywhere near his cars, refusing to give them back.

- To avoid winding up your neighbours, you could do a lot worse than to borrow a trick from cricketers in India and Pakistan, who since the 1980s have used rubber balls wrapped in brightly-coloured electrical tape. The tape can also be used to mimic the leather seam of the real thing, so you can even swerve the ball in the air like the pros.

CHAPTER THREE

THE KIT BAG

I n a knockabout game of cricket, dustbins, sticks or traffic cones can all be used as a wicket. Short of players? Simply chalk three stumps onto a wall so there's no need for a wicket-keeper. At the bowler's end, a brick or a sweater will do the job. Trapped in the office? No problem – join generations of bored workers who have whiled away the hours with a tennis ball and improvised bat, not such a far cry from the game's founders idly swinging away with their crooks in front of a gate.

For those who take their cricket seriously, however, the right equipment is not only important, but potentially life-saving.

Willow and leather

The first cricket bats were curved, with good reason. As balls were bowled underarm along the ground, batsmen swept the ball away like a hockey stick, so it made sense to have most of the weight at the bottom. Then, in the 1760s, after the laws of cricket were changed to allow bowlers to 'loop' the ball in the air, bat-maker John Small came up with a revolutionary idea – the straight bat.

Even so, there were no laws stating the shape or size of the bat until the Reigate player Thomas 'Shock' White went to the crease in 1771 carrying a bat as wide as the stumps. This weapon of mass obstruction was considered terribly unsporting, and a law was soon introduced restricting the width of the bat to four and half inches, with steel gauges used to check suspiciously large bats. Even modern manufacturers sometimes fall foul of the law: before the Zimbabwe-India game in

2003, an inspection by match referee Clive Lloyd found that several bats on both sides were too wide. Rumour has it that several players were seen busily sandpapering their bats down before the match!

Since the early 1800s, almost all cricket bats have been made from English willow, known as *Salix alba caerulea*, which is both tough and light. Strips of cane layered with rubber form the handle, which is spliced and glued into the main blade, then bound in twine and covered with a rubber grip – leading to a famous double entendre by Jonathon Agnew, who reduced fellow BBC commentator Michael Vaughan to fits of giggles with the question: 'It's not easy putting a rubber on, is it?'

> ❛ I just want to get into the middle and get the right sort of runs. ❜
>
> England batsman Robin Smith, after a nasty attack of 'Delhi Belly'

69

Bat evolution

Though the basic bat design has changed little in 200 years, there have been several innovations:

- In the 1890s, lighter bats were created by using the sapwood of the willow rather than the heartwood. These encouraged pioneering batsmen such as Ranjitsinhji to develop glancing shots that relied on timing rather than just brute strength.

- In the 1920s, Bill Ponsford was famous for his 'Big Bertha' bat, which weighed almost three pounds. Ninety years on, most bats weigh the same or more, but feel lighter due to scoops, plugs and a bowed shape that gives them the biggest possible 'sweet spot'.

- The first metal bat made its appearance in the hands of the demon Australian bowler Dennis Lillee during the first Ashes Test in 1979. Minutes later Lillee drove the ball towards the boundary with a metallic clunk. When the English captain Micheal Brearley complained that the aluminium bat was damaging the ball, the umpires agreed. After a ten minute stand-off – the bat was legal, after all – Lillee petulantly flung the offending item towards the pavilion.

- A wooden bat reinforced with a graphite strip was outlawed by the ICC after it was used by Australian captain Ricky Ponting and several other leading international players in 2006.

- Over the years, the MCC has been sent dozens of new-fangled batting contraptions for approval, including one with holes drilled into the blade for aerodynamic purposes, described by observers as a 'Swiss cheese bat'. One of the most revolutionary is the Mongoose, designed for Twenty20 cricket, which has a handle as long as the blade, creating a sweet spot twice the size of that on a traditional bat. It was first used in competition by Australian batsman Stuart Law in 2009, who called it 'a half-brick on a stick'.

1720   1750   1840   1930

The evolution of the cricket bat

The red cricket ball, or 'cherry', has changed little over centuries. It has always been regarded as an object of menace. In its first literary mention, in *The Mysteries of Love and Eloquence* (1658) by the English poet, Edward Phillips, the cricket ball is a symbol of brutality: 'Would my eyes had been beaten out with a cricket ball the day before I saw you.'

The first known makers of the ball were Duke & Son of Penhurst in Kent, established in 1760, who wound thread around a piece of cork then wrapped it in a leather case. Cricket balls are still made from a core of elastic cork, giving the ball its bounce, which is layered with tightly wound string and covered by a leather case made of four pieces stitched together with a raised sewn seam.

Following a law introduced in the 1770s, the balls used in men's cricket must weigh between 5.5 and 5.75 ounces (155.9 and 163 g), and since 1927 they must measure between $8\frac{13}{16}$ and 9 in (224 and 229 mm) in circumference. The balls used in women's and youth matches are slighter smaller. As ever in

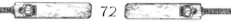

Odd balls

- White balls are used in many limited overs cricket matches, especially those played in the evening, as yellowish floodlights give red balls a brown hue that's dangerously close to the colour of the pitch. Curiously, white balls also seem to swing more than red balls, though no one is exactly sure why.

- Yellow and orange balls have also been used in evening games, while a pink ball was used for the first time in an international match in July 2009 when the England Women's team defeated Australia.

- It's illegal to apply any substance to the ball that is likely to help it swing more in the air, but once in a while balls get an accidental coating. In 1995, South African cricketer Daryll Cullinan hit a ball for six into a frying pan full of fried calamari being cooked by a group of spectators outside the boundary. Play was halted for ten minutes while the umpires waited for it to cool down enough to remove the oily coating. In the end, the ball had to be replaced as it was too slippery for the bowler to grip properly.

- In November 2004, a golden cricket ball covered in 2704 diamonds was made in Sri Lanka to celebrate the opening of a jewellery store in Australia.

cricket, the devil is in the detail. Depending on where the match is being played, different brands of ball are used. The Duke and SG brands, for instance, have a more pronounced seam than the Kookaburra, which can help spinners grip the ball better.

Shiver me timbers

Nothing brings more joy to a bowler's heart than the sight of upended stumps cartwheeling across the pitch. These three vertical posts, a.k.a. the 'poles' or 'timbers', support the two bails (crosspieces) to form a wicket at each end of the pitch. They have a spike at one end for hammering into the ground, while the other end has a groove to provide a resting place for the bails.

In the early days of the game there were just two stumps, forming a wicket that was low and broad. Their ends were forked to support the bail which easily toppled when a stump was hit. The middle stump was introduced in the late 18th century after a notorious game in 1775 when Edward 'Lumpy' Stevens bowled clean through the wicket without knocking off

74

off the bail three times in a row. Thereafter the third stump became the norm, with the exception of an exhibition match at Lord's in 1963, when a fourth stump was added. The aim was to give the bowler more to aim at, forcing the batsmen to play more attacking cricket. It didn't catch on.

Today's stumps are 28 inches high, but in the late 1820s, William Ward, MP for the City of London, came up with a cunning plan to level the odds between the mismatched Gentlemen and Players: getting the two teams to defend wickets of differing size. In 1832, the Gentlemen defended wickets 22 inches (55.9 cm) tall and 6 inches (15.2 cm) across, while the Players defended wickets 27 inches (68.6 cm) tall and 8 inches (20.3 cm) across. Even so, the Players still won with ease, and the game was forever after known as the 'Barndoor Match' or 'Ward's Folly'.

White knights

A 1743 painting of a game at the Artillery Ground in London shows two batsmen and a bowler dressed in white shirts, breeches, white, knee-length stockings and shoes with buckles, while the umpire wears a three-quarter length coat and a three-cornered hat. A century later, cricketers simply wore the latest fashions: tight white jackets, neckcloths around their throats, and matching silk stockings and gloves. By the 1850s, however, most professional teams wore coloured shirts: the All-England shirt was white with red dots.

All-white clothing, known as cricket 'whites' or 'flannels' only became the norm in the 1900s, and usually consists of trousers, shirt and V-necked jumper with coloured piping around the edge. White was chosen as it allows the red ball to be seen and is a cooling colour on a hot summer's day. All very eminently sensible, but spare a thought for those left with the job of cleaning the team kit, as getting stains out of white clothes is a nightmare. When it comes to footwear, good grip is everything. Where boots with metal

76

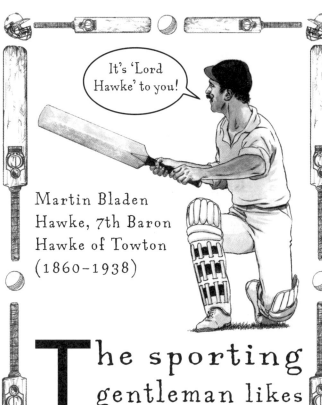

It's 'Lord Hawke' to you!

Martin Bladen Hawke, 7th Baron Hawke of Towton (1860–1938)

The sporting gentleman likes nothing better than a delicate tickle down to fine leg.

cricket spikes once did the job, modern shoes use rubber dimples to grip the turf. At the international level, whites are now only worn during Test cricket. The garish multi-coloured pyjama outfits seen in today's one-day and Twenty20 games first appeared in Kerry Packer's World Series Cricket in the late 1970s. Designed to make the game more 'fun', they are still regarded by many diehard fans as an abomination.

Last but by no means least is the cricket cap, which dates back to the 18th century. Every country has its own colour, most famous being the baggy green cricket cap of the Australian cricket team, which is often credited with mystical talisman-like properties. Shades give players a chance to stand out from the rest of the team, such as the eye-catching yellow shades worn by West Indian captain Chris Gayle in 2009. The latest sunglasses combine cool with hi-tech optics. Their lenses not only change in darkness depending on the amount of light, but filter light from the green end of the spectrum, making the red ball more visible. Today's poor-sighted cricketers usually wear contact lenses, but many great cricketers have

worn spectacles out on the pitch. Clive Lloyd, the West Indies batsman, was instantly recognisible thanks to his distinctive bottle-sized spectacles. England batsman Geoff Boycott wore glasses for the early part of his career (though he handed them over to the umpire whenever he was called upon to bowl), along with a clutch of top-class spin bowlers such as Alf Valentine, Dilip Doshi and Daniel Vettori.

The wrong trousers

In 2005, after Sri Lankan bowler Lasith Malinga terrorised his batsmen in the first Test, the New Zealand captain Stephen Fleming made an unusual request to the umpires: change your trousers! Fleming claimed that Malinga's low bowling action meant that the ball was being lost in the dark trousers of umpires Steve Bucknor and Darrell Hair. Though the trousers stayed put, both umpires agreed to remove their dark ties, while Bucknor sportingly tied a white jumper around his waist. It didn't stop Malinga claiming nine wickets and the Man of the Match award.

Leg, head and bits before wicket

There's more energy in a speeding cricket ball than there is in a hammer-head hitting a nail, so basic protection would seem like good sense. But even after the switch from underarm to the faster round-arm bowling in the mid-19th-century led to the first pads (at first made from wood), a few brave but foolhardy batsmen persisted in the notion that leg guards were for softies.

In August 1836, Alfred Mynn almost had to have his legs amputated after a long innings facing Samuel Redgate, one of the quickest bowlers in England, without protection. The horrific injuries persuaded Reverend Lord Beauclerk, president of the MCC, that pads on the legs were indispensable against fast bowling.

Cricket pads are awkward things, but a direct hit on the knee is enough to persuade the hardiest batsmen not to leave the pavilion without them. In the old days of metal clips and buckles, there was always the danger that

a pad would come loose while a batsman was halfway down the wicket. Thankfully, today's Velcro fasteners are much more reliable. While batting pads reach the lower thigh, wicket-keeping pads only protect the shins and knees, but are much easier to wear while squatting behind the wicket.

Modern batsmen, festooned in pads and gloves, are heavily armoured. Under their clothes there's also a multitude of arm pads, thick thigh guards and chest guards to protect against deliveries that kick up off the pitch. The abdominal protector, or 'box' (today a moulded plastic cup covering the soft bits between the legs), was probably first worn in the late 18th century, while the first head protection was invented in the 1930s by Patsy Hendren. The more perceptive reader might wonder why it took over 100 years for men to realise that it's also important to protect one's brain. Full helmets appeared in the late 1970s in Australia, worn by Barry Richards and Tony Greig in the World Series. At first, these were little more than motorbike helmets with visors attached.

Fast bowlers traditionally rely on a bit of 'chin music' (bowling bouncers at the head or throat) to soften up their opponents, and even the best batsmen get their fair share of direct hits. Yes, pads and helmets soften the blow, but taking a flying ball to the chest or head still hurts like hell, while a player hit in the box tends to crumple into a groaning heap.

Bruises and broken fingers are another occupational hazard for batsmen, despite wearing batting gloves that cover the fingers in a sausage-like padding. Wicket-keeping gloves are much larger, with extra padding and webbing between the fingers. Wearing gloves while fielding is banned – however cold the weather – but padding and helmets are strongly recommended for fielders in 'silly' positions close to the batsman.

Cricketing hits

- 'Soul Limbo' by Booker T and the MGs. The original BBC Test Match cricket theme and for many English fans, the sound of cricket.
- 'Dreadlock Holiday' by 10 CC. Possibly the most famous pop song about cricket. All together: 'I don't like cricket, oh no, I love it'.
- 'When An Old Cricketer Leaves The Crease' by Roy Harper. A slice of nostalgia, featuring a traditional Northern English brass band for added village ambiance.
- *The Duckworth Lewis Method.* In 2009, two Irish musicians Neil Hannon and Thomas Walsh produced the world's first concept album about cricket, named after a mathematical formula for calculating the target score for the team batting second in a one day match interrupted by weather. Highlights include a tune written from the viewpoint of England batsman Mike Gatting: 'How such a ball could be bowled I don't know but, if you ask me, if it had been a cheese roll it would never have got past me'.
- 'Enna Enna cricket' by Lahiru Perera. Despite being banned for its menacing lyrics this song became a hit in Sri Lanka in the build up to the 2011 World Cup. It threatened that the Australian team would end up as bird food while the New Zealanders, still reeling from the Christchurch earthquake, could have their jaws broken. Meanwhile English fans were told they would be defeated to badly that Buckingham Palace would cave in.

In a word

Anyone hoping to fathom the riddle wrapped in a mystery inside an enigma that is cricket should begin by learning a few essential terms:

- **Bails.** Small wooden sticks that bridge the gap between the top of the stumps. One of the bails has to fall right off for a batsman to be given 'out'.
- **Boundary.** The perimeter of the field is marked by the boundary rope laid along the ground.
- **Crease.** At both ends of the pitch is a pair of parallel white lines that mark a batsman's 'safe' ground. The inner line, or 'popping crease', is generally where the batsman stands when facing the bowling. When making a run, he must get part of his bat and/or body over this line to stay 'in'.
- **Innings.** A team's turn to bat.
- **Over.** A set of six (traditionally eight in Australia) legal deliveries bowled in a row by a bowler. Then it's all change as another bowler begins the next over from the other end of the pitch.
- **Pitch.** A narrow, 22-yard (20.1 m) long rectangular strip in the centre of the field. Also known as the 'wicket' (see below).
- **Wicket.** Rather confusingly, this has three meanings: (1) the stumps (2) the pitch and (3) a way of saying a batsman is out, as in 'Jack has taken Jill's wicket'.

CHAPTER fOUR

LET BATTLE COMMENCE

In casual games of cricket, the rules are often made up on the spot. While cruising in the Mediterranean in 1904, the crew of the British warship HMS *Irresistible* relaxed in the evening by playing cricket on deck. They fashioned bats from shark's fins while the ball was made from the bones of the yellowtail snapper fish. Any batsmen hoisting the ball overboard his whole team were given out, while guiding the ball down a nearby hatchway often produced five or six runs as it rolled onto the deck below.

In the street cricket played in Tamil Nadu state, India, the 'Double Gaaji' rule allows a batsman to bat twice if his or her side is short of players. 'Thuchees' allows for minor distractions such as a truck crossing the pitch after the ball is bowled. In Australian and England backyard games, the classic 'one hand, one bounce' rule means the batsman is out if a fielder can catch it with one hand after it has bounced once. In my old office, you were given out if you hit the ball down the stairs, where it was likely to roll past the boss's door. Invariably, the rules are constantly tweaked to allow for chance events.

Even in professional cricket, there is room for ambiguity as the game is governed by laws rather than rules, one of the reasons why playing in the 'spirit' of the game is taken so seriously. In practice, that means no skullduggery, no rough stuff, and agreeing with the umpire even if he or she is clearly as blind as a proverbial bat.

Since the MCC first laid down the laws in 1788, they have been constantly revised and updated. The most recent code, drawn up by

the ICC (the game's lawmakers since 1993), came into force in 2010. By and large, the laws are identical for men and women, so if you prefer, for every 'he' read 'she'.

Nuts and bolts

The game is usually played with two teams of eleven players a side (the number can be less or more but only eleven are allowed on the pitch at once), plus two umpires and two scorers. If a player falls ill or gets maimed during a match, a substitute, known as the 12th man, can field in their place, though he is not allowed to bat or bowl.

Each game begins with a coin toss, and the successful captain chooses whether to bat or field first. Cue thunder, lightning and a heavy downpour. The basic aim is to win, by scoring the most runs. Bowling out the opposition batsmen before they reach their target is a classic way of doing this.

As the drama unfolds, starring roles go to the batsman (anyone in the middle of the pitch holding a bat) and the bowlers, who fling the

ball at them. The bit players are the fielders dotted around the field. One batsman takes strike, while his trusty partner waits patiently at the other end for his turn and does his best to keep out of the bowler's way. Meanwhile the rest of the batting side pretend to watch the action unfold from the pavilion, while covertly texting their friends, listening to their MP3 players or inspecting their fingernails for dirt.

There must always be two (and no more) batsmen out on the pitch, so once there's only one batsmen left in, the batting team is all out. Then, like it or not, it's their turn to field and the opposing side come in to bat.

What the batsman does

All the talk of the 'gentleman's game' is little more than a fig leaf covering the naked brutality of a contest that at times evokes the bloody gladiatorial contests of ancient Rome.

The umpire gives his signal. The bowler pounds in with all the self-restraint of an axe murderer, giant strides eating up the ground,

then unleashes the ball with all his might at the waiting batsman. At the other end, the striker grips his mighty staff in both hands, tapping it nervously on the ground as he waits for the onslaught of the oncoming missile. Moments later, there's a flashing blade and... the batsman parries the ball away. So far, so good. He's kept the ball from hitting the stumps, and gets another go.

If the batsman hits the ball far enough, he and his partner run in opposite directions between the two creases to score, you've guessed it, a 'run'. If the ball keeps going, so will they. There's always the danger that a nimble-fingered fielder will scoop up the ball and fling it to either the bowler or the wicket-keeper (the gloved, often impish character usually found loitering behind the stumps). If a batsman doesn't reach the safety of the crease before the bails are whipped off, he's out. However, well-disciplined batting partners usually agree stop to running before there's a risk of this happening, and whoever is left facing the bowler takes the next ball.

Does it ever end?

In first-class matches, each team gets two innings (never 'inning'). Tests (of willpower, sanity/insert your own joke) between international sides last up to five days. There are three outcomes:

- **Win.** When one side has a higher combined total after bowling out their opponents twice.

- **Draw.** When neither team achieves this in time.

- **Tie.** If the combined score is the same when the final wicket is taken. This has only happened twice in Test matches – Australia vs West Indies in 1960, and Australia vs India in 1986.

Things that can spice up a game:

- Breaks for lunch, tea and drinks (on hot days). Will the batsman lose his concentration?

- An approaching cloud formation, which can help bowlers to swing the ball in the air.

- 'Jaffa'. An almost unplayable delivery that leaves a batsman groping hopelessly at thin air.

- Fours usually generate a ripple of applause, but hitting a ball for six is considered VERY EXCITING, especially if it soars over the pavilion.

- Antics. Bowler John Snow lobbed a ball of soap at batsman Peter Marner to liven up one dull county game. The ultimate clean delivery? The result was entered in the scorecard as: 'ball exploded'.

- Streakers on the pitch. In 1989 Sheila Nicholls ran onto Lord's cricket ground fully nude and did a cartwheel to the crowd. During a Test match in 1977, an unamused Australian cricketer Greg Chappell spanked a pitch invader with his bat.

- Shorter formats. As the clock ticks down in one-day and Twenty20 games, there is often a flurry of fours and sixes combined with a quick fall of wickets as slogging shots lead to easy catches and skittled stumps.

Against a fast bowler, a batsman has about half a second to plan and execute his shot. Even if he 'reads' what the bowler is going to do, he must gamble on the what the ball is going to do in the air and after it bounces. The ball can be hit in any direction a batsman chooses, and runs are scored whether the shot is deliberate or accidental.

Most satisfying of all is walloping the ball to the boundary. If it bounces or rolls over the line, it counts as four runs, but if the ball is flighted over the boundary rope without touching the ground, the batsman scores six runs. Either way, no running is required, allowing a batting maestro to pile on the runs without breaking a sweat.

The leisurely nature of cricket has meant that over the years the game has thrown up some unlikely heroes. The game's first star player, W. G. Grace, was a champion runner in his youth. But in later life he piled on the pounds to the point where he refused to chase the ball in the outfield. 'The ground is too far away,' he explained. The pioneering spin bowler, F. W. Lillywhite, 'couldn't get his underarm past his

belly'. (N.B. Such pie-eaters should not be confused with 'pie throwers', a nickname for poor bowlers who might as well be a clown throwing a pie.)

Weighing in at an impressive 22 stone (140 kgs), Warwick Armstrong was probably the heaviest man ever to play Test cricket. But it didn't stop him from captaining Australia to eight successive Ashes victories in the early 1920s. Other corpulent captains include Australian Mark 'Tubby' Taylor, a jack-knifing close fielder with the reflexes of a cat, and Mike 'Fat Gat' Gatting, who spearheaded the England batting line-up for 18 years.

An 1883 cartoon which shows W. G. Grace looking down upon batsman Bobby Abel, who stood at just 5 ft 4 inches (1.62 m)

How to score

- **Running between the wickets**. In theory, you can keep going indefinitely, though four is the probably the limit given the size of most grounds. In the 1930s, a pride of lions were seen circling a cricket ground in Kenya. When the ball was hit in their direction, they came to take a closer look. No fielder dared to retrieve the ball, which had stopped just inside the boundary, and, in cricketing lore the two batsmen kept running between the wickets until they collapsed in exhaustion.

- **Overthrows**, sometimes known as 'buzzers'. There's a chance for extra runs if a bumbling fielder flings the ball past the wicket-keeper, and four overthrows if the ball keeps going and crosses boundary rope. On at least four occasions in Test cricket eight runs have been scored off a single ball, most recently by Australian batsman Andrew Symonds when an overzealous New Zealand fielder threw the ball over the wicket-keeper's head.

- **Boundaries**. The quickest way to pile on the runs and whip up the crowd.

- **Bye**. A run scored when the batsman does not touch the ball with either his bat or body. Usually results from shoddy fielding behind the wicket. A leg bye is a run scored after the ball bounces off a batsman's body.

- **No Ball**. An illegal delivery, mostcommonly when a bowler is too far forward or too wide when ball is released.

- **Wide**. When a delivery is so wide of the stumps the batsman can't reach it with a normal stroke.

Five penalty runs are given for a variety of other nonsense, when a fielder:

- Deliberately scuffs the pitch to help the ball turn in the 'rough'.

- Uses something other than his body to stop the ball, even if it is accidental. In 2010 in Cape Town, South Africa were awarded five penalty runs after Graeme Swann's delivery hit England wicket-keeper Matt Prior's helmet, which was lying on the ground.

- Deliberately kicks the ball away over the ropes. Indian fielder Virender Sehwag did this in 2010, to keep the weaker batsman on strike when South Africa were one wicket away from being bowled out.

- Illegally changes the shape or surface of the ball, known as ball-tampering.

Wides, no balls, byes, leg byes and penalty runs are all tallied as 'extras' on the scorecard and are not credited to the batsman. A bowler who gives away very few extras is considered 'tidy'.

Totting it all up

Back in the day, the score was kept by marking notches on a stick. Modern scorebooks are packed with enough statistics to satisfy even the most fact-hungry, anorak-wearing fan. If you simply want to get your head around the scorelines spouted by cricket pundits, here's how it works:

Let's say the score is West Indies 530-7 declared, with Australia on 320-5 (just to be contrary, Australians will write this as 5-320). That means the West Indies have lost 7 out of a possible 10 wickets (remember that there always need to be two batsmen at the crease). They then decided to declare at 530 runs, as batting for longer might not give them enough time to bowl out the Australians. In reply, the Australians have so far made 320 runs for the loss of five wickets.

None of this actually tells you who is winning, though experienced fans will know that in this instance Australia are facing an uphill battle to pass the West indian total as most of their best batsmen are out. Additional pointers come from a plethora of computer-generated statistics and charts. The numerophobic are advised to look away:

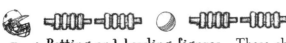

- **Batting and bowling figures.** These show how the competing batsmen and bowlers performed during an innings or match.

- **Strike rate.** How quickly a batsman scores, in runs per 100 balls. Likewise the Economy rate shows how many runs have been scored off a bowler, in runs per over.

- **The Wagon Wheel.** This shows where each scoring shot was played and so-named as it looks like an collection of spokes radiating out from the stumps. This can also be used by a captain to plot fielding tactics as you can spot where a batsman is scoring his runs.

- **The Manhattan.** This bar chart of runs per over looks like a city skyline, and gives an idea of the ebb a flow of the game.

- **The Worm.** A line graph showing the run rate plotted against the number of overs, an easy way to compare the progress of the two teams at a similar stage in the game.

The (real) Manhattan skyline

Pot-bellied batsman Arjuna Ranatunga, who led the Sri Lankan team to an unbeaten title-winning campaign at the 1996 Cricket World Cup, typically walked singles or jogged slowly for a couple of runs even if the ball was well on its way to the boundary. During one hot evening session in Sydney, he called for a runner, claiming that he had 'sprained something'. This request sparked the legendary sledge from Australian wicket-keeper Ian Healy, who muttered: 'You don't get a runner for being an overweight, unfit, fat ****!', which was picked up by the stump microphones and broadcast on television.

Thanks to sports diets and fitness regimes, the age of fat cricketers is probably over. In 2009, all-rounder (literally) Samit Patel was dropped from the England limited-overs squad after he put on too much weight. Bucking the slender trend is 20-stone Dwayne Leverock of Bermuda, famed for celebrating a stunning one-handed catch in the 2007 World Cup with his trademark 'jig'.

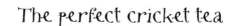

The perfect cricket tea

Whatever the weather, the highlight of an English cricket match is often the tea. Forget protein shakes, this is sports nutrition at its finest (though you might need a short nap before resuming play):

Sandwiches
Cheese and tomato
Ham and mustard
Egg and cress
Salmon and cucumber
Corned beef

Savouries
Pork pies
Sausage rolls
Quiches
Pizza slices
Samosas
Onion bhajis

Cakes
Scones and cream
Victoria sponge
Chocolate brownies
Battenburg cake
Shortbread

All washed down with lashings of tea or homemade lemonade.

Test results

According to recent research, there's no good reason to expel oversized and unfit players from the team. In 2007, a study by Australian scientists into the effects of international cricket on the body concluded that 'physical conditioning and muscle training is not going to necessarily improve your performance in cricket.' According to their analysis, during a Test century, which takes on average three and a half hours of batting, a batsman will: stand still for two hours, walk for an hour, jog for ten minutes, spend just five minutes running hard, and only about a minute and half sprinting!

There's more, proving that umpires aren't the only men in white coats to take a keen interest in the game:

- Research at the University of New South Wales found that left-handed batsmen have an advantage due to 'negative frequency dependent effect', a convoluted way of saying something you could probably guess anyway – that bowlers are less accustomed to facing left-handers.

- Boffins from Northumbria University School of Psychology and Sport Sciences revealed that helmets slowed a batsman's brain by making their heads hot. But, as they wisely pointed out, 'getting run out is preferable to brain damage'.

- In 2003, scientists in Cambridge came up with a bouncy new boot design, the Torque, with spring-loaded studs that act as mini shock-absorbers. These could potentially prevent the foot problems that shorten the playing careers of some cricketers.

- In 2006, the England team were given a masterclass on the science behind ball-tampering by Rabi Mehta, a scientist from the Fluid Mechanics Laboratory at NASA Ames Research Center in Moffet Field, California, who studies swing in wind tunnel tests.

- Slow-motion replays have revealed that unlike most ball players, cricketers tend to hit the ball sideways as it passes rather than back in the direction it came from. To hit the ball with the 'meat' of the bat, the batsman must time the shot to a few thousandths of a second.

- A fighter pilot pulling out of a dive experiences a force of about 10 gs (they're pushed with a force of ten times their weight/gravity). Without a special suit that helps circulation, they'd black out at 2 gs. Pity the poor cricket ball then, which must withstand a force of 12,000 gs when struck by a bat with full force, enough acceleration to rip a human body to shreds.

All players get to bat, however dismal they are. The opening batsmen, nos. 1 and 2 in the batting order, must face the new ball. This is hard and shiny, making it faster and more likely to bounce high off the pitch. So it's the openers' job to take the 'shine' off the new ball by playing good defensive strokes while ideally getting the scoreboard ticking over, a tactic expertly demonstrated by English batsmen Geoff Boycott and Trevor 'Barnacle' Bailey, whose repetitive blocking tactics are the stuff of legend. The next few batsmen, at nos. 3, 4 and 5 in the order, are often the best batsmen in the team and are expected to make a lot of runs. Number 3 is often the star batsman, such as Brian Lara of the West Indies or Sachin Tendulkar of India.

In the middle come the all-rounders, bowlers who can also bat, such as England's Ian Botham, India's Kapil Dev and Pakistan's Imran Khan, along with wicket-keepers who can bat such as Adam Gilchrist of Australia. Even if they are better than some of the batsmen higher in the order, putting these players at no. 6 or 7 gives them a chance to recover from a heavy bowling session or squatting behind the stumps during their opponent's innings.

Bowlers make up the lower order, or 'tail end' at nos. 8, 9, 10 and 11. More often than not, they are out for a low score. If they do post a big innings, the tail is said to have 'wagged'. The lower order batsmen also play an important role in hanging on for a draw. During the First Test in the 2009 Ashes series, England bowlers Monty Panesar and James Anderson prevented an Australian win by surviving 69 nerve-shredding balls, tormenting their rivals with a succession of smothering defensive shots.

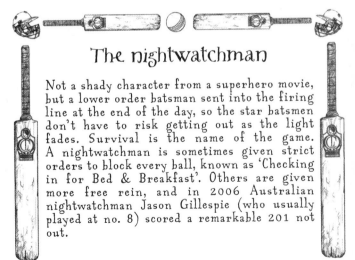

The nightwatchman

Not a shady character from a superhero movie, but a lower order batsman sent into the firing line at the end of the day, so the star batsmen don't have to risk getting out as the light fades. Survival is the name of the game. A nightwatchman is sometimes given strict orders to block every ball, known as 'Checking in for Bed & Breakfast'. Others are given more free rein, and in 2006 Australian nightwatchman Jason Gillespie (who usually played at no. 8) scored a remarkable 201 not out.

What the bowler does

Today overarm bowling is the norm. The bowler must launch the ball with a straight arm, as 'chucking' the ball with a bent elbow is banned, but he or she can pick up extra speed with a long run-up. For many years, Muttiah Muralitharan, the Sri Lankan spin bowler, was singled out for his unique action. 'Murali', arguably the best bowler of all time, was born with an elbow that prevented him from straightening his arm. The bent elbow, along with incredibly supple wrists, made it look as if he was throwing the ball as well as giving it more fizz. Muralitharan was finally cleared after a super fast camera combined with 3D motion sensing technology proved this was just an optical illusion.

There are three species of bowler: fast, medium and slow (or spin). While a spin bowler may take just a couple of steps, speed merchants such as Shoaib Akhtar have a run-up of over 40 metres, taking them a full minute to walk in between each ball. When coach Bob Woolmer asked Akhtar to cut it down, so he could bowl for longer, Akhtar refused, saying

'Can a plane take off without a run-up?' A fast bowler's momentum often carries him halfway down the pitch, providing an opportunity to glare menacingly at the batsman from close range.

Bowlers will try anything to bamboozle batsmen. Some fast bowlers rely on sheer pace, drawing gasps from the crowd as they hurl down deliveries capable of snapping a batsman's ribs. Slinging the ball directly at the batsman's head, known as a beamer, is frowned upon (and illegal). But most umpires will tolerate one or two bouncers in every over. Bowled short and fast, these intimidating deliveries kick up brutishly, forcing the batsman to duck or lean out of the way. One vicious variant is the 'throat ball', aimed at the adam's apple. More effective at taking a wicket rather than just battering the opposition is a well-placed Yorker, where the ball slides just under the bat. A tricky delivery to pull off, but almost unplayable if done well.

Medium-pace bowlers rely less on pure ooopmh and more on swerving the ball in the air, known as swing. This is done by making

the ball shiny on one side, which makes it more rough on the air. Ready for some more science? The different textures force air to pass over the two sides at different speeds, causing a pressure difference, and hey presto, the ball swings. You may have noticed that bowlers keep rubbing the ball against their trousers, often near to the groin. This is simply an age-old way of keeping one side polished, often with the help of spit.

A particular breed of fast and medium-pace bowlers are known as seamers, such as Australian Glenn McGrath and New Zealander Richard Hadlee. They specialise in landing the ball on its seam, resulting in an unpredictable bounce or a delivery that veers away from the batsman.

> **6Endless cricket, like endless anything else, simply grinds you down.9**
>
> Ted Dexter, English cricketer

Verbal mishits

Commentators beware – cricketing terms can quickly get you into deep water. King of the cricketing blooper must surely be BBC commentator Brian Johnston, who gamely announced (as England batsman Peter Willey faced West Indian paceman Michael Holding): 'The bowler's Holding, the batsman's Willey'.

Other memorable Johnston gaffs include:
- 'There's Neil Harvey standing at leg slip with his legs wide apart, waiting for a tickle.'
- 'Welcome to Worcester where you've just missed seeing Barry Richards hitting one of Basil D'Oliveira's balls clean out of the ground.'
- Ray Illingworth has just relieved himself at the pavilion end.

There's more:
- 'If England lose now, they will be leaving the field with their heads between their legs!' – Geoffrey Boycott
- 'His throw went absolutely nowhere near where it was going.' – Richie Benaud
- 'I think he thinks he's better than he is, and I think he's right' – Geoffrey Boycott
- 'David Boon is now completely clean-shaven, except for his moustache' – Graham Dawson
- 'Yorkshire 232 all out, Hutton ill – I'm sorry, Hutton 111.' – John Snagge, BBC News
- 'That slow motion doesn't show how fast the ball was travelling.' – Richie Benaud

Thrice bowled

The hat-trick got its name after All-England player H. H. Stephenson became the first player to get three wickets in three consecutive balls at Sheffield's Hyde Park ground in 1858. In those days, any outstanding sporting feat resulted in a collection among the spectators, and the money was used to buy Stephenson a white hat.

- Only one player has taken two hat-tricks in the same Test match: English leg spinner Jimmy Matthews, in 1912, playing against South Africa.

- In 2007, Sri Lankan bowler Lasith Malinga became the only player to take four wickets in four balls in an international match, during a one-day game.

❛ I know one thing for sure. West Indian bowlers like it young and hard. ❜

Commentator Rameez Raja
(referring to the ball during
a one day international)

Where fast bowlers are all huff and puff, spinners rely on guile and digital dexterity. There are two main sub-species. Off-spinners like to use their fingers to spin the ball so it turns in towards a right-handed batsman. Leg-spinners also twist their wrist as they release the ball, causing it to bounce away from a right-handed batsman.

In the Victorian era, spin-bowling was regarded by some as a devilish act not worthy of a gentleman, and even today there's a hint of the dark arts about it, probably because the ball can seem to be doing one thing and then do the complete opposite. A slow ball floated down the pitch looks oh-so-innocent. The batsman strides confidently up the pitch, licking his lips in anticipation. As it bounces, however, the ball turns viciously. The batsman swipes wildly and misses, or mishits the ball, gifting a catch to a nearby fielder.

A slow ball that's too short or long is quickly punished and dispatched to the boundary. But it's a risk most spin bowlers are willing to take. On the right pitch where there is plenty of 'bite', they can win a match single-handed.

During the Fourth Ashes Test in 1956, Jim Laker took a remarkable 19 wickets (out of a possible 20) for just 90 runs.

Spinners are innovators as well as gamblers, always on the hunt for a new trick. Today, bowlers like Ajantha Mendis and Ravichandran Ashwin are mesmerising batsmen with the 'carrom', where the ball is squeezed out of the hand by flicking it between the thumb and a bent middle finger, a technique that allows them to spin it either way.

Finally, mention should go to ambidextrous Sri Lankan bowler Hashan Tillakaratne. During a match against Kenya during the 1995-96 World Cup, he bowled three deliveries of his only over with his right arm, then switched to his left for the remaining three, a tactic occasionally employed by the extrovert Australian bowler Colin 'Funky' Miller (who famously bowled with blue hair in a Test match against the West Indies in 2001).

Up the wizard's sleeve

Something wicked this way comes:

- **Googly** (also known as a 'Wrong 'un' in Australia). A cunning change of wrist action by a leg-spinner that spins the ball the opposite way. When this was first unleashed by Bernard Bosanquet in 1900, batsmen complained it went against the spirit of the game because they couldn't tell which way the ball was about to spin.
- **Chinaman**. A similar delivery by a left-arm bowler. The term possibly gets its name from a racist remark made by an English batsman after a delivery by Ellis 'Puss' Achong, a West Indian bowler with Chinese parentage, got him out during a match at Old Trafford, Manchester in 1933.
- **Doosra**. A Hindi word describing an off-spinner's version of the googly, delivered out of the back of the hand.
- **Flipper**. Invented by the Australian leg-spinner Charlie Grimmett, this was spin maestro Shane Warne's trademark delivery. Back spin, caused by pinching the ball as it is bowled, makes it skid through lower and faster than expected.
- **Drifter or Floater**. A delivery bowled by an offspinner which curves away from a right-hander, then carries straight on instead of turning.
- **Flighted ball**. Top spin makes the ball hang in the air before dropping sharply.

Out in the field

While not as glamourous as bowlers and batsmen, fielders do a variety of useful jobs:

- Chasing after the ball
- Catching the ball
- Running out a batsmen with a well-aimed throw.
- Screaming like howler monkeys at an LBW decision.
- Trying not to look bored while waiting for the ball to come vaguely in their direction.

With the bowler at one end of the pitch and the wicket-keeper at the other, the captain has to find places for the other nine players to stand. While captaining the New South Wales side, Keith Miller would set his field by simply by saying, 'OK fellas, scatter'. Most captains, however, arrange the field to suit the speed and style of the bowler and the weaknesses of the batsmen. When the ball or batsman is new, fielders stand closer in, to intimidate the opposition. But once the batsman has his eye in (or the bowlers run out of steam), they usually stand further back to save more runs.

Busiest of the fielders is the wicket-keeper, who does all of the stumping and much of the catching and needs to keep a sharp eye on the ball if it fizzes past the stumps. If it evades his grasp, the batsmen can set off for a run known as a 'bye'. For a spinner, the wicket-keeper often stands close to the stumps so he can whip the bails off if the batsmen is lured out of his crease.

For a share of the limelight, a fielder's best bet is to leap like a salmon and snatch the ball from mid-air for a glorious catch. Not all catches are made with the hands though. In 2009, Warwickshire close fielder Jonathon Trott leapt into the air to avoid a ball hit by Sussex batsman Ed Joyce. When he landed, he found the ball lodged snugly into his right trouser pocket – a fair catch. In 1947, England fast bowler Alf Gover caught a ball with his knees while wriggling out of his cricket jumper. In the second Test against India at Kanpur in 1959, Neil Harvey was fielding close to the wicket when Nari Contractor pulled a ball in his direction. Instinctively, Harvey turned and ducked, while the ball got locked between his thighs. Contractor shook his head in disbelief and trudged back to the pavilion.

Where should I stand?

The names of some fielding positions are easy to decipher. Square leg, for instance, is square to the stumps, while places with a 'silly' in them indicate the danger of standing so close to the batsman. Other positions, however, have titles that range from the obscure to the bizarre. 'Short backward square' is forever linked to the tubby Tasmanian batsman David Boon, also known as the 'keg on legs' due to his drinking habits.

Main fielding positions for a right-handed batsman

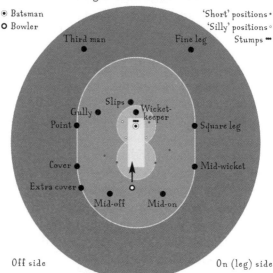

- ● Batsman
- ○ Bowler

'Short' positions •
'Silly' positions ○
Stumps ▬

Third man

Fine leg

Slips

Wicket-keeper

Gully

Point

Square leg

Cover

Mid-wicket

Extra cover

Mid-off

Mid-on

Off side

On (leg) side

All together now

Now we've met all the participants, here's how they interact. There are ten or so ways to get a batsman out. The five most common ways for a batsman to lose his wicket are:

- **Bowled.** The bowler hits the wicket with the ball (even if it hits the striker's bat or body en route), making at least one bail fall off.

- **Caught.** If a bowled ball hits the batsman's bat or glove and is then caught by a fielder before it hits the ground. If a bowler makes the catch off his own bowling it's listed as 'caught and bowled'.

- **LBW (Leg Before Wicket).** When the batsman blocks a ball that would have otherwise hit the wicket with any part of his body (normally the leg), usually accompanied by a deafening roar of the bowler and close fielders screaming 'HOWZAT!' ('how is that', i.e. is he out?) at the umpire. One of the hardest decisions an umpire has to take. In 1961, when Gloucestershire captain Tom Pugh ducked to avoid a low full toss, it broke his jaw. He was still given out LBW.

- **Run out.** Knocking the bails off while the batsman is running between the wickets. Often a dramatic moment as the batsman dives

full-length for the crease with outstretched bat at the same instant as the ball strikes the stumps after a dazzling piece of fielding. Also a cause for some major onfield strops if one batsman pushes for a run and the other doesn't, leaving the former stranded.

- **Stumped.** If the batsman steps outside his crease, e.g. to meet a delivery which he then misses, the wicket-keeper can 'stump' him by knocking of the bails with the ball in his hand.

The other ways of getting out are all pretty rare. Most common is a 'hit wicket', when an unbalanced batsman, stumbles and knocks the bails off with own bat or body. In 1921, Australia's Ted McDonald dismissed South African Billy Zulch by breaking the batsman's bat. The fragments knocked off a bail, and Zulch was given out 'hit wicket'. In 2007, England batsman Kevin Pietersen was given out after a delivery from West Indian bowler Dwayne Bravo broke the chin-strap on his helmet and knocked it onto the stumps.

Handling the ball or hitting it twice will also get you out (except to stop a moving ball hitting the wicket), as well as deliberately

obstructing fielders. In May 1919, in a match between Somerset and Sussex, batsman Harold Heygate became the first ever cricketer to be timed out after taking more than two minutes to crawl to the crease. It seems a bit harsh given that he had acute rheumatism.

Note that a batsman doesn't have to leave the field until he is given out by the umpire, though 'walking' is seen as good form in many countries. In 2011, Sachin Tendulkar won plaudits after deciding to head for the pavilion against the West Indies despite umpire Steve Davis signalling not out. In contrast, W. G. Grace famously stayed put even when the bails had been toppled, while English batting legend Colin Cowdrey was known as a 'selective walker'.

> **❝ The only time an Australian walks is when his car runs out of petrol. ❞**
>
> Barry Richards,
> South African cricketer

In the know

At this point, the cricket novice will hopefully be a little more familiar with how the game is played. To feel at ease among cricket aficionados, however, it's worth being armed with a few key statistics to help you differentiate between the humdrum and a truly exceptional performance.

Teams

- **Highest total:** 952-6 declared by Sri Lanka playing India in 1997 in the Ranasinghe Premadasa Stadium, Colombo.
- **Lowest total:** 26 all out, by New Zealand against England in 1955 in Eden Park, Auckland.
- **Greatest winning margin:** 675 runs. In 1928–29, when England (521 & 342-8 declared) beat Australia (122 & 66) at the Oval, London.
- **Narrowest win:** In 1992–3, West Indies (252 & 146) beat Australia (213 & 184) by just one run at the Adelaide Oval.
- **Most runs in the fourth (final) innings to win:** In 2002, West Indies scored 418-7 to win the match after chasing the Australian total at the Antigua Recreation Ground, St. John's.
- **Most games won:** Australia have won 341 out of 729 matches since they took part in the first Test in 1877, giving them a win rate of over 46 per cent (11 per cent more than their closest rivals England).

Batting

- **Highest score**: In 2004, Brian Lara (West Indies) scored 400 not out against England at the Antigua Recreation Ground, St. John's.
- **Most runs in a career** (to July 2011): Sachin Tendulkar (India) scored 14,692 runs in 177 matches.
- **Highest batting average**: Donald Bradman (Australia) scored 6,996 runs in 80 innings, giving an average of 99.94.
- **Most 100s**: Sachin Tendulkar (India) has hit 51 centuries.
- **Fastest 100**: Viv Richards smashed 100 runs in just 56 balls against England at the Antigua Recreation Ground, St. John's.
- **Biggest partnership**: 624 runs, shared between the Sri Lankan players Kumar Sangakkara (287) and Mahela Jayawardene (374) against South Africa at the Sinhalese Sports Club Ground, Colombo in 2006.

❝ Statistics are like bikinis... what they reveal is suggestive, what they hide is essential. ❞

Former India Test batsman
Navjot Singh Sidhu.

In the know
(continued)

Bowling

- **Most wickets in an innings**: In 1956, Jim Laker (England) took all 10 Australian wickets during their second innings at Old Trafford, Manchester, for just 53 runs.
- **Most wickets in a career**: Muttiah Muralitharan (Sri Lanka) took 800 wickets in 133 matches, including 22 10-wicket hauls (a record) and 67 matches where he took 5 wickets (another record).
- **Lowest bowling average**: George Lohmann (England) took 112 wickets at a cost of 1205 runs during the 1880s, giving an average of 10.75.

Fielding

- **Most catches in a career** (to July 2011, excluding wicket-keepers): 202 by Rahul Dravid (India) in 152 matches.
- **Most dismissals** (to July 2011): 518 (496 catches + 22 stumpings), by Mark Boucher (Australia) in 138 matches.

N.B. All figures are given for international Test matches.

Cricket chants

The raucous band of travelling English supporters known as The Barmy Army are famous for their chants. Most rely on endless repetition, rather than razor-sharp wit, to wind up the opposition (usually Australia):

> Yesterday, Ponting's troubles seemed so
>   far away,
> Now Nathan Hauritz is here to stay,
> McGrath and Warne were Yesterday,
> Suddenly, they're not half the team they
>   used to be,
> Will he lose Ashes number three,
> Yesterday came suddenly.
>
> (to the tune of The Beatles' 'Yesterday')

> He's fat
> He's round
> He bounces on the ground
> Shane Warne, Shane Warne.
>
> (to the tune of 'Olé Olé Olé')

Meanwhile, lavish praise is heaped upon England's cricketing heroes:

> Ian Bell, Ian Bell, fifty on the way,
> Oh what fun it is to see the aussies lose
>   today, HEY!
> Ian Bell, Ian Bell, give us another ton,
> Oh what fun it is to see convicts on the run.
>
> (to the tune of 'Jingle Bells')

Cricketing minnows?

Cricket is now played in 105 countries around the world. Rising stars to watch include:

- **Afghanistan.** Since the Taliban allowed the sport to be played again in 2000, the national team has gone from strength to strength. It played its first ODI in 2009, against Scotland, and rose five divisions in two years to appear in the 2010 Twenty20 World Cup.
- **Ireland.** In 2007, angry Pakistani cricket fans took to the streets in protest after their side's shock defeat to Ireland (on St Patrick's day) at the World Cup. Ireland went one better in the 2011 competition, beating the old enemy England by three wickets despite bookmakers offering odds of 150-1 against.
- **Kenya.** Kenya hit the headlines with a win over the West Indies in the 1996 World Cup, then progressed to the semi final in 2003, a remarkable achievement for a non-Test nation.
- **China.** The Shanghai Cricket Club played against many touring sides in the late 19th and early 20th centuries. Though the decidedly bourgeois association with gentlemen meant cricket was unlikely to be the sport of choice for Communist cadres, the game has undergone a revival in the last five or so years. Indeed, the Chinese Cricket Association has ambitious plans to have have 20,000 players and 2,000 coaches by 2015 and to qualify for the World Cup by 2019. Watch this space!

CHAPTER FIVE

POLITICS

As we've already seen, cricket comes in many guises. The pinnacle of the game is the Test, an international match that lasts a maximum of five days, played by a select group of ten nations recognised by the ICC: Australia, Bangladesh, England, India, New Zealand, Pakistan, South Africa, Sri Lanka, the West Indies and Zimbabwe. Play lasts for roughly 6 hours each day, or 90 overs, and each team has two innings (these end when the whole team is out or the captain declares).

The next rung on the ladder is first-class cricket, the domestic competitions found in most cricketing nations, such as the Currie Cup in South Africa, the Sheffield Shield in Australia, the Ranji Trophy in India and the Plunket Shield in New Zealand. These matches last from three to five days. In many respects these games are very similar to test cricket. The biggest domestic league is the County Championship in England, currently with 18 teams.

In the late fifties, declining gates for the County Championship led to the first one-day games, which are played over anything from 40 to 65 overs. The first official competition was the Gillette Cup, which began in England in 1963. One-day internationals (ODI), first played in the early 1970s, are often played as part of a tour that includes Test matches, or as part of a knockout competition such as the World Cup or the ICC Champions trophy.

The games last 50 overs. Some begin at 2 pm and last into the night. As well as the white balls and coloured playing kit, differences to Test matches include a 10-over limit for

bowlers and restriction on the number of players in the outfield at various stages of the game.

Twenty20 is like a one-day international on speed, with just 20 overs per innings and with all the razzmatazz of an American Football game. It's over in just three or so hours, which brings the game closer to other popular team sports and makes it a lot more TV-friendly (though purists moan that the format reduces the game to a slogging match).

It was first played at a professional level in England 2003, and in the early years of the game spectators were lured by the promise of bouncy castles, rodeos and sky-divers as well as knockabout cricket. The format spread quickly around the world (New Zealand already had its own version, Cricket Max, a 10-over game developed by former captain Martin Crowe), and in 2007 South Africa hosted the first Twenty20 World Cup. The Twenty20 tournament in India, known as the Indian Premier League, has attracted many of the world's top cricketers, with average salaries topping £2.5 million.

Roving players

While most teams have a permanent home, there is also a tradition in cricket of 'wandering clubs', nomadic teams without their own home ground. Perhaps the most famous are the I Zingari (meaning 'the Gypsies' in Italian), amateur cricket clubs formed in England and Australia in 1845 and 1888 respectively. With a motto of 'out of darkness, through fire, into light', members are expected to follow a curious set of club rules:

- keep your promise
- keep your temper
- keep your wicket up
- the Entrance fee be nothing and the Annual Subscription do not exceed the Entrance

The 'I Zingari' logo

Gentlemen and Players

Cricket is a wonderful game, but, like many sports, it has a few skeletons in the closet. The fact that there are so few Test nations underlines cricket's elitist image even in the 21st century. For decades, cricket clubs were ruled by 'them and us' attitudes, with the toffs (sometimes referred to as the blazerati) keeping out the plebs.

On the field, cricketers were divided into 'Gentleman' (public school-educated amateurs) and 'Player' (working-class professionals). In the Victorian era, the Gentlemen got bigger changing rooms, better lunches and a choice of ends. There was outrage in 1898 when Warwickshire batsman Willie Quaife, a Player, walked up the centre steps of the pavilion at Leyton in Essex after he was dismissed – professionals were supposed to go round the side.

Yorkshireman Len Hutton began a revolution in 1952 when he became the first Player to be selected as England captain (even then it was an act of desperation after 20 years of Ashes

defeat for teams led by Gentlemen). In those days, whistling down a mine shaft for a cricketer was a legend based on truth – Harold Larwood, Fred Trueman and Frank Tyson all came from mining communities – and some critics have even linked the present-day dearth of English fast bowlers to the collapse of the mining industry.

' It's a funny kind of month, October. For the really keen cricket fan, it's when you realise that your wife left you in May. '

Denis Norden,
British television writer and compère

 128

Born and bred

Yorkshire Cricket Club was formed in 1863, and until 1992 only players born in the county could play for the team. Despite this unique selection policy, Yorkshire is the most successful club in the history of English cricket, boasting an incredible 34 county championships while producing a string of great players for England such as Sir Len Hutton, Herbert Sutcliffe, Fred Trueman, Brian Close, Ray Illingworth, Geoffrey Boycott and Michael Vaughan.

This success is probably due to the high standards of League cricket in the county, which are incredibly competitive thanks to fierce local rivalries. In 1974, there was uproar when the district of Saddleworth became part of the borough of Oldham in Lancashire (Yorkshire's traditional arch rival). After bitter complaints, the rules for selection were changed so that boys born in Saddleworth could still play for Yorkshire.

Such elitism was replicated in clubs across the world, from Ceylon (now Sri Lanka) and the West Indies to Hong Kong. The MCC, essentially a private members' club, is a notorious bastion of snobbery. Only in 1998 did the club vote to open its doors to a very limited number of female members, even though women have played the game since at least the 14th century.

Ladies' firsts

The first known women's match was recorded in *The Reading Mercury* on 26 July 1745, played between 'eleven maids of Bramley and eleven maids of Hambledon, all dressed in white. The Bramley maids had blue ribbons and the Hambledon maids red ribbons on their heads'.

Matches were often between villages or teams of married and single women. They were rowdy affairs watched by 2,000 spectators or more, and like the men's game, betting on the outcome was popular (prizes ranged from barrels of ale to pairs of lace gloves).

Your bum looks big in that.

At least it distracts from your face.

Victorian lady cricketers relished the niceties of cricket etiquette.

The first women's county match was played between Surrey and Hampshire in 1811. It was sponsored by two noblemen who put forward the sum of 1,000 guineas. Legend has it that around this time the round-arm bowling action was pioneered by Christina Willes, to avoid getting her arm tangled in her wide skirt (though her brother John got all the credit after trying to get the action recognised in the men's game).

The first women's club, the White Heather Club, was formed in 1887 by eight noblewomen, who were joined by 50 others in just four years. Three years later, two professional teams known as the Original English Lady Cricketers toured the country playing exhibition matches. Their first game, in Liverpool, was watched by 15,000 spectators. The teams were very successful for two years, until their manager ran off with the profits.

Women's cricket didn't really take off, however, until the formation of the Women's Cricket Association in 1926. It organised matches across England and by 1938, over 120 clubs had joined up. The first Women's Test match, between England and Australia, was played in December 1934 over three days (extended to four days in 1985). Three years earlier, the Australian Women's Cricket Council (AWCC) had been formed to develop the game at the national level, though women and girls had been playing the game since 1874, with organised competitions at state level since the early 1900s.

The first women's World Cup was held in 1973 (two years before the men's event), thanks to campaigning by the England skipper Rachael Heyhoe-Flint. The first woman to hit a six in a Test match, in 1963, she epitomised the women's game for over a generation.

Fifty years on, women's cricket is still regarded as a bit of a sideshow, getting very little media coverage, apart from the habit of cricket camera operators in seeking out

good-looking female spectators during lulls in play. In 2009, for example, English women's team held on to their Ashes title, won the World Cup in Australia and the Twenty20 World Cup, but got very few headlines.

Things are changing – but very slowly. In May 2003, Claire Taylor became the first woman to commentate on a male Test match, and in 2009 she was declared one of Wisden's five cricketers of the year, after scoring more than 1,000 runs in 15 Tests, including 156 not out, the highest ODI score made at Lord's by a man or woman.

> ❛Professional coaching is a man trying to get you to keep your legs together when other men have spent a lifetime trying to get them apart.❜
>
> England cricketer
> Rachael Heyhoe-Flint

Cricket 'whites'

Along with snobbery and sexism, racism has also reared its ugly head over the years. In the heyday of the British Empire, cricket was seen as a civilising influence, with local children encouraged to play this 'gentleman's game' rather than traditional games.

Despite such attitudes, there was no colour bar back in England (unlike American baseball), though non-white cricketers were rare enough in Victorian and Edwardian times. The hard-hitting Indian cricketer Ahsan-ul-Haq played for the posh Hampstead club and even the MCC in 1902, while the mixed-race player Charlie Llewellyn, who became South Africa's first non-white cricketer, played 300 times for Hampshire, though perhaps only because he was able to pass himself off as white (Wilfred Rhodes described him as 'like a rather sunburned English player').

Perhaps the most famous non-white player of the Victorian era was Kumar Shri Ranjitsinhji (who made the most of his 'exotic' Eastern

135

background by claiming to be an Indian prince). Nicknamed 'Ranji' and 'Ramsgate Jimmy', he was such a favourite with the crowds that in 1896-7 there was even talk of him standing as an MP.

Throughout this period there were also international tours by non-white teams, such as the Parsi touring teams in late 1880s. The pioneering cricketer C. A. Olliviere played over 100 matches for Derbyshire after touring England with the first West Indies team in 1900.

Illustration of K. S. Ranjitsinhji, from *Vanity Fair*, August 1897

The original tourists

From the early 1860s onwards, cricket matches were played between Aborigines and European settlers on the cattle stations of western Victoria, Australia where many Aborigines worked. Spotting their natural talent for the game (and realising the novelty value of an all-black team), a group of entrepreneurs put together a side to tour England and in 1868, an Aboriginal cricket team became the first organised group of Australian cricketers to travel overseas.

The first match, played at The Oval in London, attracted 20,000 spectators. Many were drawn by curiosity as much as cricket, and the promoters were happy to play up to racial stereotypes. At the end of each game, the Aborigines put on exhibitions of boomerang and spear throwing. One member of the party, Dick-a-Dick, invited people to hurl cricket balls at him which he defended with a shield. For all the showmanship, the team contained several fine cricketers, particularly the outstanding all-rounder Johnny Mullagh. After playing against him, the England fast bowler George Tarrant admitted 'I have never bowled to a better batsman.'

In the colonies, meanwhile, English ex-pats formed exclusively all-white cricket clubs, like the Bombay and Poona Gymkhana sides of the 1900s. Talented but non-white players were also kept off teams at club and national levels. In the 1930s, George Headley, considered one of the best batsmen ever to play for West Indies, was passed over as captain because he was black (though in 1948 he finally got the job, for just one match). In Australia, the lightning-quick pace bowler Eddie Gilbert, an Aborigine and the only bowler to ever knock the bat out of the hands of the legendary Don Bradman, was repeatedly left out of the national team.

Over the years, non-white players have also suffered racist abuse from crowds – West Indian captain Viv Richards was shocked by the reception his team got touring in Australia – and sadly the problem lingers on, with Indian supporters taunting Australia's mixed-race batsman Andrew Symonds during two matches in 2007.

The apartheid system in South Africa meant that for many years the country fielded an all-white team. As a result, South Africa was excluded from Test cricket (and other international sports) in 1971. After a decade in the wilderness, standards began to drop, so the head of the South African Cricket Union, Dr Ali Bacher, decided to break the boycott by organising unofficial Tests against 'rebel' players.

The first tour, in 1982, was made by an English team led by Graham Gooch. When they landed in South Africa and announced their plans for the first time in public, there was national outrage in Britain and the players were branded the 'dirty dozen'. All were given three-year bans, and some, like Geoffrey Boycott, never played for their country again. This didn't stop further tours by Sri Lankan, West Indian and Australian players who were tempted by the handsome fees on offer. While the West Indian players got a life ban, the Australian squad, led by former Test captain Kim Hughes, were labelled 'traitors' by their Prime Minister Bob Hawke. The final rebel tour, led by Mike Gatting in 1990, was perhaps the most ill-

judged, as it showed support for the apartheid government at a time when the country was in the middle of great change (Nelson Mandela was released from prison a month after the tourists arrived). Whereas previous rebel tours had been given a warm welcome, crowds of angry demonstrators greeted Gatting's squad.

Politics and cricket have collided on several other occasions. In 1999, Shiv Sena, a Hindu extremist movement, threatened to release poisonous snakes onto the outfield to prevent India playing Muslim Pakistan. Though the campaign was called off, the Delhi police hired 30 snake charmers to patrol the stands just to be on the safe side.

Without doubt, however, cricket's darkest day was 3 March 2009. As the Sri Lankan team travelled to a match against Pakistan in Lahore, 12 terrorist gunmen armed with assault rifles, hand grenades and a rocket launcher attacked their bus, wounding seven players and killing six policemen and two bystanders in a shoot-out that lasted half an hour.

flashpoints

Thankfully, most cricket battles have taken place on the pitch. Some of the greatest clashes have occurred in games between cricket's oldest rivals, England and Australia. Experts quibble over the best Ashes ever. In 1948, an Australian side led by Donald Bradman were nicknamed 'The Invincibles' after crushing England in a 4-0 defeat. The nerve-shredding 1981 Ashes was Ian Botham's finest hour and in 2005, an inexperienced England team defied the odds to beat an Australian team packed with legends such as Shane Warne, Glenn McGrath and Ricky Ponting.

For sheer controversy, however, you can't beat the notorious 'Bodyline' Series of 1932-33, when English bowlers deliberately bowled short-pitched balls to counter the brilliance of the great Australian batsman, Donald Bradman. They aimed for the head and chest rather than the wicket, hoping to get a deflection that might be caught.

The win-at-all-costs attitude of the English captain Douglas Jardine only made matters worse. When batsman Bill Woodfull bent over in agony after English bowler Harold Larwood struck him over the heart, Jardine congratulated him with a 'Well bowled, Harold'. Later Australian wicket-keeper Bert Oldfield collapsed on the pitch and had to be carried off the field after a ball from Larwood ricocheted off his bat onto his temple.

Enraged Australian spectators almost jumped the fence to attack the English players, and only the intervention of the police prevented a riot. The feeling was mutual. Jardine spat towards the crowd while fielding close to the boundary, and told his men to call Bradman 'the little bastard.' England eventually won the series 4-1, but the resulting ill feelings between Australian and English players lasted for decades.

Though the fierce rivalry between Pakistan and India has meant long periods of the two teams refusing to play each other, when they do meet, fireworks are guaranteed. In the First Test of a two-match series in 1999, a

Creatures of habit

The rule book states that the best cricket officials are the ones that go unnoticed. Maybe in theory…

- **Harold 'Dickie' Bird** (England). Arguably the most famous umpire in the history of the game, marked out by his flat white cap and with a reputation for stopping play for weather.

- **Steve Bucknor** (West Indies). Nicknamed 'slow death' after the slow and deliberate way he raised a finger to give batsmen out.

- **David Shepherd** (England). Known for balancing on one leg when the score reached 111, traditionally regarded by English cricketers as an unlucky number. This is known as a Nelson, as in legend the English admiral only had 'One Eye, One Arm, One Leg' due to injuries in battle (in reality he never lost a leg).

- **Frank Chester** (England). One of the first umpires to stoop low as he believed it made LBW decisions more accurate.

- **'Billy' Bowden** (New Zealand). Something of a showman, he is best known for his 'crooked finger of doom', the result of arthritis, and his hop-on-one-leg-and-reach-for-the-sky signal for a six.

superb innings of 136 by Indian hero Sachin Tendulkar couldn't stop Pakistan winning the match. India got their revenge in the next game, however, when Anil Kumble captured all 10 wickets in Pakistan's second innings, leaving the series all square.

Other classic encounters include India's fightback in 2001 when they scored 657-7 in their second innings then bowled Australia out for 212 runs, for a remarkable victory, and the West Indies narrow victory over Australia in 1999 after a brilliant innings by Brian Lara.

In the hot seat

One of cricket's ugliest moments came on a hot day in Faislabad in 1987. Umpire Shakoor Rana had already been annoyed by England captain Mike Gatting's mutterings about 'One rule for one and one rule for another' after failing to give an LBW decision. Then Rana noticed shadows from England's close fielders were putting Pakistan's batsmen off, so he issued a warning to Gatting. Later, realising that one of his fielders had got too close, Gatting waved the player back.

144

Suddenly, while a ball from the England bowler Eddie Hemmings sailed through the air, Rana shouted out: 'Stop, stop!' He then accused Gatting of cheating. The England captain responded by telling Rana to get on with the game as he was within his rights to signal to his players. At this point, Rana walked off and let out a stream of foul language along the lines of: 'You're a cheating so-and-so'.

Gatting snapped. He ran up to Rana and started wagging his finger (poking it at his chest), and swore at the umpire. The incident soon hit the front pages worldwide. That night, Rana demanded an apology while Gatting steadfastly refused unless he got one in return. With both sides digging their heels in, play was cancelled for the following day. In the end, Gatting was persuaded to apologise. The match was drawn, but England lost the series 1-0.

6 You're regarded as a soft guy in Holland if you play cricket. They think it's all eating lunch and tea, and pretty boring. 9

Andre van Troost, Dutch cricketer

6 Cricket is a tough and terrible rough unscrupulous game. No wonder our American friends do not like it. 9

From a speech given by English writer
A. P. Herbert at a Surrey County Cricket
Club dinner

CHAPTER SIX

NO HOLDS BARRED

Believe it or not, despite all that standing around in immaculately-laundered whites, cricket is dirty, dangerous and hard work. And it's getting harder. Some experts claim that our warming planet will lead to an increase in skin cancer, heat exhaustion and dehydration – and that's just among the crowd.

At the beginning of the 1993 tour to the West Indies, England cricketer Chris Lewis foolishly decided to shave his hair off then headed out into the mid-day sun without a sunhat. Bad

move. 'Chris Lewis baldly went where no other cricketer has gone before,' proclaimed the Sun newspaper, 'and the prat without a hat spent two days in bed with sunstroke.'

Bowling produces large amounts of stress to the spine, leading to a plethora of ailments, bone abnormalities and dodgy discs. Fast bowlers suffer more than most from back problems that can recur unexpectedly. England all-rounder Derek Pringle once pulled out on the morning of a Test with a back strain after writing a letter – he had aggravated an old injury by leaning back in his chair.

The game's speedsters also have to endure throbbing fingers, caused by splitting the skin from repeatedly dragging it across the seam of the ball. The bones in their feet also get a mashing. England paceman Darren Gough had special boots made to ease the pain.

Wicket-keepers can develop arthritis in their knees from all that squatting, while other cricketers are liable to impingement syndrome, degenerative rotator cuff injuries and tearing of the supraspinatus tendon. I

have no idea what these are, but they all sound very painful. No wonder a masseur is an essential member of a touring party. In 2004, there was almost a player revolt prior to the England tour of the West Indies, when the English Cricket board refused to pay for the team's preferred masseuse, Vicki Byrne.

Crunch time!

There are no prizes for guessing that the worst cricketing injuries are caused by a flying 'cherry'. In 1963, in the days before body protection, English batsman Brian Close took hit after hit on the chest and ribs while facing a formidable West Indies pace attack at Lord's. His torso, black and blue from the battering, made the front pages the next day.

In 1975, English fast bowler Peter Lever caught Ewen Chatfield on the temple, knocking him out, Luckily, the English physio realised Chatfield had swallowed his tongue and ran onto the field, reviving the player with a heart massage. Australian batsman Rick McCosker had his jaw broken by England's Bob Willis in the first innings of the Centenary

Test in 1977. No one expected him to play on, but with his broken jaw wired and bandaged, McCosker doggedly came out to bat for an hour and a half in the second innings, scoring vital runs to help Australia win.

In 1986, Mike Gatting's nose was broken by a bouncer from West Indian flyer Malcolm Marshall. The ball then dropped onto Gatting's stumps, adding 'out' to injury. It was returned to the bowler with a piece of bone still embedded in it. Even helmets are no guarantee of safety. Twice in one year, 2003, Zimbabwean cricketer Mark Vermeulean suffered skull fractures due to balls squeezing under the peak of his helmet. The second injury was so bad his skull had to be sliced open to fit three titanium plates.

Other nasty incidents include a cricketer hit on the head by a crash-landing hang-glider in 1998, while in 1887, fielder Alexander Croome almost died after he impaled himself on the boundary railings while trying to leap over them. When team mate W. G. Grace tried to pull him off, the blood gushed out in torrents until Croome's wound was finally sewn up.

It gets worse. Several players have died from on-field injuries in first-class matches. In 1870, batsman George Summers died from a blow to the head, as did Karachi wicket-keeper Abdul Aziz in 1959, aged just 17, and in 1998 Indian Test cricketer Raman Lamba died after being hit in the head while fielding close in without a helmet.

Sneaky tactics

Now you know that cricket can sometimes be a matter of life or death, you won't be surprised to learn that not all players play according to the 'spirit of the game'. Some cricketers are just plain rude, like South African pace bowler Andre Nel, who stuck out his tongue at West Indian batsman Chris Gayle after dismissing him during a Test match in 2003. Others, meanwhile, will do almost anything to secure victory.

Top of the list for unspeakable cricket acts on the field is 'Trevor's Trundler'. In a one-day game in 1981, the Australian captain, Greg Chappell instructed his bowler (and younger brother) Trevor Chappell to deliver the last

A danger to others

In 2006, accountant Chris Hurd was flabbergasted when he was stopped for carrying a cricket ball on the London underground, after a policewoman told him it was a potentially lethal weapon. If the following stories are anything to go by, the officer may have had a point:

- In 2009, a veteran cricket umpire died during a league game in South Wales after failing to see a ball thrown by a fielder from about 40 metres away.

- In May 2011, a four-month-old baby escaped serious injury after being hit on the head by a stray cricket ball in Darfield, South Yorkshire. Little Theo Manderson was struck by a ball that went for six, bounced over the pavilion wall, and flew through the open door of his home.

- The same year, a 13-year-old cricket spectator was killed after a cricket ball hit him in the chest in Shahjahanpur, India.

- In 2011, cricket commentator Edward Bevan was hit by a ball for the third time while up in the commentary box.

ball underarm along the ground. Such a delivery gave the opposition batsman no chance of scoring a six off the last ball, which would have won New Zealand the match. Though technically within the law, the ploy was described by former Australian captain Richie Benaud as 'one of the worst things I have ever seen done on a cricket field.'

Next up is Dwayne Bravo's claim that he had taken a catch to dismiss England batsman Michael Yardy during a Champions Trophy match for West Indies in 2006, though video replays showed the ball clearly hit the ground first. Was it an honest mistake or pure gamesmanship?

In theory, polishing, drying or removing mud from a cricket ball are the only things a player can legally do to keep one side shiny and the other rough. But over the years, sly cricketers have found a myriad ways to 'improve' the ball, mainly to help their bowlers swing the ball better in the air. Common techniques include rubbing the ball on the ground, scuffing it using bottle tops and other devices sneakily hidden inside pockets, or tampering with the seam.

In the 1940s, Australian bowler Keith Miller used to pass a hand through his Brylcreemed hair so that he could apply a greasy coating to the shiny side of ball. Thirty years later, during an English tour of India in 1976-7, John Lever was accused of rubbing vaseline on his head before each session, then applying this to the side of the ball.

Things really came to a head in the 1990s. First, Pakistan's fast bowlers were accused of fiddling with the seam to achieve large amounts of reverse swing. In the 1970s, the Pakistani bowler Sarfraz Nawaz learned how to get an older, worn ball to swerve a considerable distance in the air, but the opposite way to how you would expect. Teammate Imran Khan passed this devastating bowling technique, called 'reverse swing', onto the next generation of players, including Wasim Akram and Waqar Younis, in the late 1980s.

Pakistan's bowlers were cleared of all charges, but two years later England captain Michael Atherton was accused of ball tampering during the Test match with South Africa at

Lord's, after television cameras caught him reaching into his pocket and then smearing something on the ball. Atherton claimed he was merely rubbing dust on to the ball to... er, 'maintain its dry and rough condition', but was fined £2,000 for 'failing to disclose the dirt' to the match referee.

A decade later, in January 2004, India's Rahul Dravid was alo fined after he was spotted rubbing a cough lozenge onto the shiny side of the white ball during a one-day international against Zimbabwe. The following year, during the Ashes, England's bowlers managed to create reverse swing early on by applying saliva that had been sweetened by sucking on fresh-breath mints.

Less subtle was the approach used by Pakistan's all-rounder Shahid Afridi in 2010, who got a two-match ban after being caught on camera biting the ball to change the seam. In a radio interview, Afridi claimed he was simply 'smelling' the ball, but eventually pleaded guilty.

A war of words

Winding up rivals at the crease with whispered insults, known as sledging, is another favourite tactic, and nobody does it better than the Australians. Some comments are aimed at the opposing batsman's ability, like Australian fast bowler Merv Hughes's quip to England batsman Robin Smith, 'Mate, if you turn the bat over, you'll see the instructions on the back.' Other jibes are more personal. When Ian Botham came to the crease during an Ashes match, Australian wicket-keeper Rodney Marsh welcomed him with the line: 'So how's your wife and my kids?'.

The traffic isn't all one-way. During the 1991 Adelaide Test, Javed Miandad called Merv Hughes a 'fat bus conductor'. A few balls later, having dismissed Miandad, Hughes called out 'Tickets please' as he jogged past the departing batsman. Aussie paceman Glenn McGrath also met his match when he tried to goad Zimbabwe no. 11 Eddo Brandes, saying, 'Why are you so fat?', only to get the retort: 'Because every time I make love to your wife, she gives me a biscuit'.

Sometimes actions speak louder than words. One of the best ripostes came courtesy of West Indian big hitter Viv Richards. After zipping the ball past Richards' flailing bat a couple of times, Glamorgan bowler Greg Thomas taunted him with the line: 'It's red, round and weighs about five ounces, in case you were wondering'. Richards replied by hoisting Thomas' next delivery clean out of the ground. 'Greg, you know what it looks like,' said Richards. 'Now go and find it.'

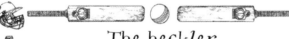

The heckler

When it comes to heckling, spectators also get to join in the fun. Stephen Gascoigne, known as Yabba, was a regular at the Sydney Cricket Ground, where he would sit on a grassy patch known as 'The Hill' and fire jibes such as:

- 'I wish you were a statue and I were a pigeon.'
- 'Send 'im down a piano, see if 'e can play that!'
- 'Your length's lousy but you bowl a good width!'
- 'Leave our flies alone, they're the only friends you've got!', to English captain Douglas Jardine during the ill-tempered 'Bodyline' series of 1932–33.

Smoke, spooks and bungs

Shenanigans also take place off the field. It was rumoured that when Lancashire or the Australians were batting at Yorkshire's ground at Bramall Lane in Sheffield, the nearby steel forges deliberately stoked up their chimneys to help the Yorkshire team. Another kind of smoke may have affected Australian performances in 1964, when Holland recorded its first victory over a Test nation after taking the touring party on a trip to a Dutch 'coffee shop' the night before. The Australian squad was also on the receiving end of scare tactics in their 2005 Ashes tour, when several of the players were spooked by the ghost of a 14th-century nobleman in an old hotel in Durham.

Far more serious is the match-fixing that has dogged the game throughout its history. During England's 1998-99 Ashes tour, it emerged that Mark Waugh and Shane Warne had been secretly fined in 1995 for giving information to an Indian bookmaker in Sri Lanka (ironically they had previously accused Pakistani cricket captain Saleem Malik of trying to bribe them to lose matches). Perhaps the most celebrated case

of match-fixing in modern times is that of South African cricket captain Hansie Cronje. In 2000, the vice squad in Delhi tape-recorded a conversation proving that Cronje had accepted bribes totalling about £65,000 from another Indian bookie to throw matches. In the resulting inquiry, Cronje also pointed the finger at Saleem Malik of Pakistan and India's batting star Mohammed Azharuddin, who received bans along with Cronje (who died in a plane crash in 2002). Several other South African players were also implicated, and the affair cast a shadow over the whole sport.

During Pakistan's 2010 tour of England, further allegations were made that three Pakistani players, Mohammad Asif, Mohammad Amir and Salman Butt, had accepted bribes to deliberately bowl no-balls at specific points during the 4th Test at Lord's. This enabled gamblers with inside knowledge to make very specific bets, known as spot-fixing. Though Asif, Amir and Butt protested their innocence, all three were banned from international cricket for several years. The huge sums bet on matches, especially in Asia, mean that the problem is unlikely to go away.

Cricket in the arts

Given cricket's enormous potential as a metaphor for life's trials and tribulations, it's surprising how few artists have mined this rich seam:

- **Movies.** Hollywood has yet to produce an epic cricketing movie. But in 2001, the blockbuster Bollywood movie *Lagaan* depicted a remote village taken on their ruthless British rulers in a game of cricket, while in *Iqbal* (2005) a poor lad beats the odds to play cricket for his country.

- **Documentary.** *Out of the Ashes* (2009). The astonishing story of the Afghani cricket team who almost qualified for the 2011 World Cup the despite the fact that there wasn't a single cricket pitch in their war-torn home country.

- **Novels.** *Netherland* (2008) is a book about cricket, set in New York. Whatever next? Yet this tale of a Dutchman playing at the Staten Island Cricket Club in the wake of 9/11 was on President Obama's bedside table in 2009.

- **Science Fiction.** In Douglas Adam's novel *Life, the Universe and Everything*, the Wikkit Gate is a symbol of the basic ideals of civilisation, while cricket is a tasteless reminder of the Krikkit Wars in which a supernova bomb (a red cricket-ball shaped weapon of mass destruction) destroys the entire universe.

- **Literary inspiration**. Warwickshire fast bowler Percy Jeeves gave P.G. Wodehouse the name for his famous butler. Wodehouse was a keen cricketer who played in a team with fellow writers A. A. Milne (creator of *Winnie-the-Pooh*), Jerome K. Jerome (*Three Men in a Boat*) and Arthur Conan Doyle (*Sherlock Holmes*) in the Allahakbarries, a team captained by J.M Barrie (*Peter Pan*) from 1887 to 1913.

- **Poems**. When Victorian all-rounder Alfred Mynn, the 'Lion of Kent', died in 1861, William Jeffrey Prowse wrote a poem in his memory. The last six lines run:

> *With his tall and stately presence, with his nobly moulded form,*
>
> *His broad hand was ever open, his brave heart was ever warm;*
>
> *All were proud of him, all loved him. As the changing seasons pass,*
>
> *As our champion lies a-sleeping underneath the Kentish grass,*
>
> *Proudly, sadly will we name him - to forget him were a sin.*
>
> *Lightly lie the turf upon thee, kind and manly Alfred Mynn!*

161

Harold
Larwood
(1904–1995),
English bowler

Don Bradman
(1908–2001),
Australian
batsman

CHAPTER SEVEN

THE GREAT PLAYERS

Many cricket matches are won by outstanding performances by individual players, so it's only fitting that we end our whistlestop tour of the game by looking at some of the finest players ever to pull on a pair of cricket trousers. Selecting a single Greatest Ever XI is an almost impossible task, so what follows is a shortlist of worthy candidates from all countries and all eras.

163

The Batsmen

Sir Don Bradman (Australia)
In 100 years time, the 'Don' will probably still be regarded as the greatest batsman of all time. He claimed his skill came from hitting a golf ball with a stump against a wall as a teenager. In his first test, at the age of 22, Bradman scored 974 runs in the series, including the then record innings of 334 runs. He continued this incredible form to end his career with a stellar batting average of 99.94 runs per innings. To put this in perspective, Brian Lara, in 2nd place, has an average of 52.88. Bradman played his final Test in 1948, at the age of 40. For such a rock-solid player, it seems only fitting that his favourite food was rice pudding.

Brian Lara (West Indies)
The tenth of eleven children, left-hander Lara will always be remembered for two innings in particular: his 400 not out for West Indies against England at Antigua in 2004, and his 501 not out for Warwickshire against Durham, the highest individual score in first-class cricket. To add to this, in a single over

during a Test match against South Africa in 2003, Lara, known as 'The Prince', scored a record 28 runs off Robin Peterson of South Africa. His daughter Sydney is named after the city where he scored his first Test hundred, a stunning innings of 277 runs.

Sachin Tendulkar (India)

To improve the young Tendulkar's concentration, coach Ramakant Achrekar placed a one-rupee coin on the top of the stumps, saying that any bowler who could dismiss him would get the coin. If Tendulkar lasted the whole session without losing his wicket, he kept the coin (he eventually won 13). He made his Test debut at 16 and scored his first century a year later. Combining a flawless technique with raw aggression, Tendulkar holds the records for the most runs scored, the most hundreds and the most fifties in Test and ODIs, and is the only player to score 200 runs in a ODI. Tendulkar has also appeared in more Test matches than any other player – 177 – and as he grew older he incorporated several new strokes into his repertoire. Curiously, though he bats, bowls and throws with his right hand, he writes with his left hand.

Sir Viv Richards (West Indies)

Stylish, powerful and fearless (Richards never wore a helmet), the 'Master Blaster' still holds the record for the fastest Test century, described by English bowler John Emburey as 'the biggest carnage I have ever seen in such a short space of time in any first-class game'. An excellent fielder and a useful off-spin bowler, in 1987 he also became the first player to score a hundred and take five wickets in a ODI. Known for his swaggering batting style, Richards was the first person ever to play both World Cup cricket and football (as part of the Antigua team he appeared in qualifying matches for the 1974 World Cup).

Sir Jack Hobbs (England)

Often referred to as 'The Master', Hobbs first played cricket for a church choir team. He is widely regarded as the best opening batsman of all time, forming a famous partnership with Herbert Sutcliffe. In a career lasting from 1905–1934, he remains the leading scorer in scored first-class cricket, with over 61,000 runs, and the batsmen with the most hundreds (197). Once asked how he kept fit during the

winter, Hobbs replied he preferred ballroom dancing as it was good for his footwork. (In recent years, former England cricketers Mark Ramprakash and Darren Gough both showed similarly nimble feet in winning the English TV show, *Strictly Come Dancing*.)

Sunil Gavaskar (India)

A battling player who was particularly effective against fast bowlers, 'Sunny' was the first batsman to score 10,000 runs. If you believe his autobiography, he almost ended up catching fish rather than cricket balls. Shortly after Gavaskar was born, his uncle noticed a curious little hole near the top of his left ear lobe. The next day, the eagle-eyed relative was horrified to find that the hole had vanished. After a frantic search of the hospital, little Sunny was found sleeping next to a fisherwoman. Nurses had mistakenly swapped the two babies after their bath.

Big and small

Cricketers come in all shapes and sizes. The tallest player to play first-class cricket is the Pakistani bowler Mohammed Irfan, standing a lofty 2.16 m tall. Other notable giants include:

- Curtley Ambrose (West Indies) – 2 m
- Joel Garner (West Indies) – 2.03 m
- Bob Willis (England) – 1.9 m
- Courtney Walsh (West Indies) – 1.97 m
- Glenn McGrath (Australia) – 1.9 m
- Chris Tremlett (England) – 2.01 m
- Jacob Oram (New Zealand) – 1.9 m

The shortest Test player ever is the Bangladeshi wicket-keeper Mushfiqur Rahim, at 1.5 m tall.

Other tiny titans are:

- George 'Tiny' Wells (England) – 1.57 m
- Alfred Percy 'Tich' Freeman (England) – 1.57 m
- Parthiv Patel (India) – 1.6 m
- Tatenda Taibu (Zimbabwe) – 1.65 m
- Sachin Tendulkar (India) – 1.65 m
- Aravinda de Silva (Sri Lanka) 1.61 m

W. G. Grace (England)

16-year-old William Gilbert Grace played his debut first-class match in 1865, and was still playing a record-equalling 44 seasons later in 1908. After scoring 224 not out for an All-England playing against Surrey in 1866, he rapidly became the world's first cricket superstar. A showman who attracted huge crowds to the game, 'WG's trademark bushy beard made him instantly recognisable. Although a brilliant batsman, he also used his immense popularity to bully other players and umpires alike. In one match, after being bowled first ball, he casually placed the bails back on top of the stumps, dismissing the umpire's complaints with a haughty, 'Don't be silly, they've come to watch me bat, not you umpire'.

> ❛Dr W. G. Grace
> Had hair all over his face.
> Lord! How all the people cheered,
> When a ball got lost in his beard.❜

E. C. Bentley, English novelist and humourist

The bowlers

Muttiah Muralitharan (India)
Though his early career was plagued by accusations of 'chucking' – Michael Holding, the former West Indian fast bowler, called it a 'javelin throw' – the 'Smiling Assassin' went on to become the most successful Test match bowler ever. He holds a hatful of bowling records, including the most wickets in both Test cricket and in ODIs (averaging over six wickets per Test), as well as one batting record – for the most ducks in international cricket (59 in total).

Shane Warne (Australia)
The first cricketer to take 700 Test wickets, Warne single-handedly made the dying art of leg-spin popular again, thanks to an assortment of balls that drifted in, sloped out, or fizzed low and hard toward the stumps. He was no mean batsman, either, scoring 3,000 runs in Test cricket. During the 1993 Ashes series, Warne famously did Mike Gatting like a kipper with a viciously turning delivery dubbed the 'ball of the century'. Afterwards Graham Gooch quipped, 'He [Gatting]

looked as though someone had just nicked his lunch.' Off the field, Warne was rarely out of the headlines, thanks to a string of affairs, his beer belly, and a scandal over the use of diet pills containing banned substances.

Glenn McGrath (Australia)
When his New South Wales teammate Brad McNamara first saw McGrath's skinny white legs, he said, 'You've stolen a pigeon's legs', and the nickname 'Pigeon' stuck. Relying on relentless accuracy rather than raw speed, the Australian paceman became the leading wicket-taker among fast bowlers in Test cricket, with 563 wickets in a career that spanned 14 years. He often took the scalps of big-name batsman, dismissing Michael Atherton 19 times and Brian Lara on 13 occasions. His stubborn determination is summed up in a story told by Steve Waugh. Once so bored out of his mind at a caravan park south of Sydney, McGrath decided to walk into town, despite having no idea how far away it was. He returned six hours later, tired but content.

Nicknames

Cricket has a long tradition of using nicknames. Some are kinder than others:

- Trevor Bailey – 'The Boil' or 'Barnacle'
- Paul Adams – 'The frog in a blender' (due to his unusual bowling action)
- Stephen Harmison – 'GBH' (Grievous Bodily Harmison)
- Imran Khan – 'The Lion of Lahore'
- Harbhajan Singh – 'The Turbanator'
- Ian Botham – 'Beefy'
- Joel Garner – 'Big Bird'
- Merv Hughes – 'Fruitfly'
- Michael Holding – 'Whispering death'

Malcolm Marshall (West Indies)

Marshall was the fast bowler that no batsman wanted to face. Fast, devastatingly accurate, and owner of the deadliest bouncer on the planet, Marshall could also swing the ball well or make it leap off the seam on dusty batting tracks. In all, he took 376 Test wickets at a phenomenal strike rate of a wicket every 46 balls. During a match against England in 1984, Marshall broke his left thumb while fielding. After bravely batting one-handed, he then bowled with his left hand wrapped in plaster, ignoring the pain to take 7 for 53.

Wasim Akram (Pakistan)

The 'Sultan of Swing' was possibly the best left-arm fast bowler of all time, and together with Waqar Younis formed one of the most successful bowling partnerships in cricketing history (cryptically known as 'the two Ws'). His unique run-up meant that he shielded the ball from the batsman until the very last moment. Akram was also one of the pioneers of reverse swing bowling, claiming over 916 international wickets, including 414 in Tests. In a deadly spell during the 1992 World Cup final, he dismissed the English batsmen Allan Lamb and Chris Lewis with two 'unplayable' balls in a row.

Talented all-rounder Chris Lewis was nicknamed the 'prat in the hat' after shaving his head before a Test match and getting sunstroke.

All-rounders

Sir Gary Sobers (West Indies)

Born with an extra finger on each hand (removed at birth), the young Sobers played golf, soccer and basketball for Barbados before becoming the greatest all-rounder cricket has ever seen. He made his Test debut after just two first-class matches, aged 17, and broke the record for the highest Test score – 365 runs – at 21. The first player to hit six sixes off an over, Sobers claimed 235 Test match wickets as well as scoring 8,000 Test match runs.

Kapil Dev (India)

The only player in the history of cricket to have taken more than 400 wickets and scored more than 5,000 runs, it's no wonder that the 'Haryana Hurricane' was voted India's cricketer of the century in 2002. Dev is an all-rounder in more ways than one. Author, coach, restaurant owner and honorary colonel in the Indian army, he has appeared in adverts promoting everything from shaving cream and life insurance to motorbikes and TVs, as well as starring in four Bollywood films.

Sir Richard Hadlee (New Zealand)

Hadlee was the nearest thing to a one-man team you'll get, a hard-hitting batsman and the first cricketer to break through the 400-wicket barrier. Highlights include his 15-wicket haul against Australia at Brisbane in 1985–86 and figures of 5 for 53 during his last ever Test match, against England in 1990. Despite his destruction of several England batting line-ups, he became the first cricketer to be knighted while still a player.

Just as memorable as the great cricket performances are the larger-than-life characters that populate the game, whether fiery pacemen like Dennis Lillee and Merv Hughes, curmudgeonly Yorkshiremen such as Fred Trueman and Geoff Boycott, or bad boys like former Indian captain Sourav Ganguly, hauled over the coals by the game's governing body a record 12 times, and England bowler Phil Tufnell, disciplined for numerous offences to do with women, drink, drugs and all-round offensive behaviour.

What *larks*!

- During the inaugural World Cup in 1975, India's former wicket-keeper Farokh Engineer offered to give all-rounder Abid Ali a lift to the game at the Headingley ground in Leeds. Just a few minutes before play was due to begin, a furious Abid stomped into the Indian dressing room. On the way, Engineer had asked him to hop out and buy him a newspaper, then drove off, leaving Abid to make his own way to the ground.

- In 1991, the England players David Gower and John Morris got in hot water after buzzing the pitch in a Tiger Moth biplane while their team-mates were still at the crease.

- England all-rounder Andrew 'Freddie' Flintoff decided to go one better during the World Cup in 2007. After leaving a nightclub close to the team's hotel in St Lucia, Flintoff climbed into a pedalo in the dark, then had to be rescued after falling off it.

- In 2007, England's cricketers wound up the overweight Zaheer Khan by leaving jelly beans scattered around the wicket during the drinks interval. One of the chief suspects, Alastair Cook, protested his innocence, 'I am also disappointed to find myself accused in some quarters of supplying the offending sweets, particularly as I am a Fruit Pastille man myself'.

In a game for eccentrics, England wicket-keeper Jack Russell takes some beating. Never seen without wearing his battered old flowerpot sunhat or trademark black wicket-keeping gloves on the field, he:

- Washed his own kit in his room, then hung it over the nearest lamp to dry.

- Drove between games with a cut-out sleeping bag over his legs to avoid getting a chill. He also had a block fitted under the accelerator, to avoid over-stretching his Achilles tendon.

- Drank 20 cups of tea a day. After dipping the tea bag in once, he hung it on a nail ready for the next cuppa. According to former England bowler Derek Randall, Russell once used the same bag for a whole Test match (that's around 100 cups).

- Said he wanted his hands to be amputated after his death and preserved in formaldehyde.

Popular but obsessive South African cricketer Neil McKenzie's pre-match rituals involved taping his bat to the ceiling and insisting that all toilet seats in the dressing room were down before going out to bat. In the context of a game like cricket, however, such behaviour doesn't seem so extraordinary.

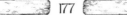

If all this still seems a little strange, don't worry, you're in good company. As American film director Jim Jarmusch once said:

❝ Cricket makes no sense to me. I find it beautiful to watch and I like that they break for tea... My friends from The Clash tried to explain it years and years ago, but I didn't understand what they were talking about. ❞

  178

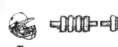

Appendices

Well-worn phrases

To show your familiarity with the game, pep up your observations with the following old chestnuts:

- 'He took the aerial route' (hit the ball over the fielders)
- 'It's a good batting track' (an easy wicket for batsmen)
- 'He's gone without troubling the scorer' (got out for 0 runs, known as a 'duck')
- 'They bat a long way down' (a team with good tail end batsmen)
- 'He was beaten all ends up' (when a batsman is completely bamboozled by a good delivery)
- 'A heave-ho/cow corner/agricultural swipe/rustic blow' (a big slog, often employed by tail enders with nothing to lose at the end of an innings).
- 'Plumb' (When the ball hits a batsman on the leg directly in front of the stumps – a sure LBW)
- 'He gave it the maker's name' (used the full face of the bat to play a shot)
- 'Tickled round the corner' (when the batsman gently steers the ball behind the wicket)
- 'That's fairly raced away/gone like a rocket to the fence' (when the ball is hit hard to the boundary)
- 'He's given that the full treatment' (a hefty blow)

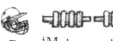

- 'Metronomic/with Glenn McGrath-like precision' (a very consistent bowler)
- Young bowlers are 'raw', fast bowlers are often 'snarling' or 'fearsome', spinners 'wily' or 'mesmeric', medium-pacers 'naggingly accurate', Asian batsmen 'wristy' and cover drives either 'silky' or 'scorching'.
- 'The long walk to the pavilion' (is it ever short? After a batsman has been dismissed)

Everyone for cricket?

- French cricket. A classic party game with just one batsman, whose legs are the 'stumps'. The aim of the game is to stay 'in' as long as possible, while the other players try to get the batsman 'out' by hitting his or her legs (usually below the knee) or by catching the ball after it's hit. Usually played with a tennis ball, to save the legs from a battering. The name is probably a slur on the French, age-old rivals of the English, like the cricketing term a 'French cut', a woeful stroke where the batsman clips the ball with his inside edge and misses hitting his own stumps by a few centimetres.
- Beach or backyard cricket. Casual variants played almost anywhere that's not intended for the game. Every version has its own rules depending on the location, such as 'no slogging' (when there aren't enough fielders), 'six and out' (a big hit into the sea or over a hedge and you're out) and 'tip and run' (if you hit the ball, you have to run). In

 180

1934, if you believe the story, a game was taking place on a beach in Sohar in the Sultanate of Oman when a ball struck into the briny was swallowed by a passing shark. The umpire gave the batsman out, entering 'caught Fish bowled Burkitt Ullah' into the scorebook.

- Indoor cricket. Around since the late 1960s, this variant has a formal set of rules. It is usually played on specially-designed courts surrounded by string nets, between two teams of eight players, who must each bowl 2 overs and bat for 4 overs in an inning of 16 overs. A good indoor batsman makes good use of the 'slap shot', hitting the ball hard into the ground so that it bounces above the opposing fielders and into the netting for an automatic score.
- Kwik cricket. A fast and furious version of the game designed to introduce the sport to children, using a plastic bat and ball.

Cricket lingo

Cricket has long trumpeted its ethos of 'fair play' (once prompting Henry VIII to call it the 'sport of kings', though it's worth remembering that his version of fair play involved lopping off the head of anyone who got in his way). Over the years, the game's values and jargon have crept into wider usage:

- It's just not cricket – unfair or unjust
- A sticky wicket – an awkward situation
- Knocked for six – something that leaves you

devastated or completely speechless
- To play a straight bat – handling something in a correct or felicitous manner
- To go into bat for – to lend someone your support
- To field – to handle something (e.g. a question)
- On the back foot – in defensive mode
- To 'up stumps' – to stop doing something or to uproot yourself
- A good innings – a good, long life

British Prime Minister Margaret Thatcher liked to use cricketing comparisons to make herself look like one of the boys, saying that:

- She wouldn't 'duck the bouncers' over European monetary reform.
- She would 'hit the bowling all round the ground' after her disgruntled deputy, Sir Geoffrey Howe, accused her of undermining her own government like a captain 'breaking the team's bats before they went to the wicket'.

Cricket machines

The umpire's job is a thankless one. The man in the middle has to make tough decisions over events that happen in the blink of an eye, knowing full well that the smallest error of judgement will be seized upon by disgruntled players, fuming fans and know-it-all commentators. These days, a range of hi-tech toys play their part in the debate:

- **Hot Spot** is an infrared imaging system used to determine whether the ball has struck the batsman, bat or pad.
- **Hawk-eye.** Originally used for brain surgery and tracking missiles, this employs six TV cameras set up at different angles around the pitch to follow the path of the ball from the instant it leaves the bowler's hand. It is used when LBW decisions are referred to the Third Umpire.
- **Snick-o-Meter.** 'Snicko' is a highly sensitive microphone located in one of the stumps, which can pick up the sound when the ball nicks the bat. At present, umpires don't get to use it.
- **Speed gun.** This uses radar technology to measure how fast the ball is moving after it leaves the bowler's hands (by reflecting radio waves off it).
- **Stump Vision.** A small camera fitted onto the stump that gives a stump-eye view of the playing field. When South Africa captain Andrew Hudson grabbed the middle stump after his team's victory in a 1992 World Cup match, he forgot about stump camera and ripped up 10 metres of cable!

Cricket timeline

1598 Game of 'creckett' mentioned during court case at Guildford, Surrey (England).

1624 Jasper Vinall becomes the first person known to be killed playing cricket.

1706 First detailed description of the game written by William Goldwin in his poem *In Certamen Pilae*.

1709 First match between two county sides (in England) – Kent vs Surrey.

1744 First version of the laws created at London Club, Artillery Grounds, Finsbury.

1769 First recorded cricket century, scored by John Minishull for the Duke of Dorset's XI.

1771 Bat width set at 4½ inches.

1775 Middle stump introduced.

1788 Marylebone Cricket Club (MCC) issues the first authoritative version of the laws.

1792 Calcutta Cricket Club formed in India (the oldest surviving cricket club outside the British Isles).

1803 First recorded cricket match in Australia, in Sydney.

1814 Earliest known match played at Lord's Cricket Ground, the present home of MCC.

1820s Use of wicket-keeping gloves first mentioned.

1835 Round-arm bowling made legal by MCC.

1830s Batsmen allowed to wear pads.

1844 First international match, United States vs Canada.

1851 Tasmania vs Victoria, earliest first-class game in Australia.

1864 Overarm bowling becomes legal.

1877 First recognised Test match played between England and Australia in Melbourne.

1882–3 'Ashes' first used to describe Test series played between England and Australia.

1884 Boundaries introduced.

1889 Test between England and South Africa is first not involving Australia. Currie Cup also founded.

1890 County Championship formalised in England.

1892–3 Sheffield Shield first held in Australia.

1900 Six-ball over introduced in England (was five). Cricket appears in Olympics for first and only time.

1909 ICC is founded (then Imperial Cricket Conference, now International Cricket Council).

1928 West Indies plays first Test, vs England at Lord's.

1930 New Zealand Test debut vs England.

1932 India's first ever Test match, vs England at Lord's.

1932–3 'Bodyline' Ashes series takes place in Australia.

1934–5 Ranji trophy held for first time in India. First Women's Test match, England vs Australia.

1948 All Test matches now maximum of five days' long.

1952 Pakistan plays first Test, vs India in Delhi.

1963 First one-day knockout tournament, in England.

1968 First one-day league tournament, in England.

1970–91 South Africa banned from international cricket.

1971 First one-day international, England vs Australia.

1973 First Women's World Cup held.

1975 First Cricket World Cup, held in England.

1977 Kerry Packer creates World Series Cricket, signing over 50 Test players and revolutionising one-day game.

1982 Sri Lanka's Test debut, vs England.

2000 Bangladesh's first Test match, vs India in Dhaka.

2003 First-class Twenty20 match played for first time.

2007 First Twenty20 World Cup.

2011 Three top Pakistani cricketers jailed after plotting to cheat in a match against England.

Glossary

All-rounder A player who can bat *and* bowl well.

Ashes Test series between England and Australia.

Bails Small wooden sticks that bridge the gap between the top of the stumps.

Ball tampering Illegally changing the ball's condition.

Beamer A full toss bowled at head height. Illegal!

Bouncer A short-pitched ball that reaches the batsman at chest or head height.

Boundary The perimeter of a cricket field (marked by a rope laid along the ground), or when a batsman scores a four or a six.

Box Abdominal (groin) protector worn by batsmen.

Bye A run scored when the batsman does not touch the ball with either his bat or body.

Century When a batsman scores at least 100 runs.

Crease A pair of parallel white lines that mark a batsman's 'safe' ground at each end of the wicket.

Declaration When a batting side finishes their innings before all their players are out.

Delivery A ball that has been bowled.

Duck A score of 0. A golden duck is a first-ball dismissal.

Extras Any runs not scored by batsmen: byes, leg byes, wides, no-balls and penalty runs.

Full toss A ball that reaches the batsman without bouncing.

Hat-trick When a bowler takes a wicket in three consecutive deliveries.

Innings. A team's turn to bat. In a Test match, each team gets two innings (weather permitting).

Leg bye A run scored when the ball deflects off the pad and the batsmen run.

GLOSSARY

Leg-side The area of the pitch behind the batsman's legs.
For the right-handed batsman, the left half of the pitch.

Maiden An over in which no runs are scored off the
bat, and no wides or no-balls are bowled.

MCC Marylebone Cricket Club, the spiritual home of
cricket at Lord's ground in London.

Nightwatchman A tailender sent in near the end of a
day's play to protect more valuable batsmen.

No-ball An illegal delivery, usually when the bowler
has overstepped on the front crease.

Off-side The side of the pitch a batsman's body faces.
For the right-handed batsman, the right half of the pitch.

One-day International (ODI) Limited overs match
played in a single day or day/evening sessions.

Over Six legal deliveries bowled in a row by a bowler.

Pitch A narrow 22-yard (20.1 m) long rectangular strip
in the centre of the field. Also called the 'wicket'.

Run-rate The average number of runs scored per over.

Seam The ridge of stitching holding the ball together.
Can be used make the ball bounce unexpectedly.

Sledging Verbal abuse used to put off a batsman.

Swing When a ball swerves through the air.

Tailender Lower-order batsman, e.g. nos. 8. 9, 10 and 11.

Twelfth man Substitute fielder (who can't bat or bowl).

Twenty20 Modern, fast-paced variant of the game
lasting just 20 overs per innings.

Umpire The two (or three) enforcers of the laws (two
on the pitch and a third with access to video replays).

Wicket (1) The pitch (2) the stumps and bails, or (3)
when a bowler gets a batsman dismissed.

Wide A delivery that lands so wide of the stumps it's
impossible to score off it with a normal stroke.

Index

INDEX

INDEX

Sept 2, 1882.

THE SPORTING TIMES

In Affectionate Remembrance

OF

ENGLISH CRICKET,

WHICH DIED AT THE OVAL

ON

29th AUGUST, 1882,

Deeply lamented by a large circle of sorrowing
friends and acquaintances.

R. I. P.

N.B.—The body will be cremated and the
ashes taken to Australia.